"He is not here;
he has risen, just as he said."

MATTHEW 28:6

FROM THE
GRAVE

A 40-Day Lent Devotional

A. W. TOZER

MOODY PUBLISHERS

CHICAGO

Edited by Kevin Emmert
Interior and cover design: Erik M. Peterson
Coverimage: copyright © by Link Creative /Lightstock. All rights reserved.

Library of Congress Cataloging-in-Publication Data

Names: Tozer, A. W. (Aiden Wilson), 1897-1963, author.
Title: From the grave : a 40-day Lent devotional / A. W. Tozer.
Description: CHICAGO : MOODY PUBLISHERS, 2017.
Identifiers: LCCN 2016041478 (print) Ɏ LCCN 2016044047 (ebook)
Ɏ ISBN 9780802415097 Ɏ ISBN 9780802495228
Subjects: LCSH: Lent.
Classification: LCC BV85 .T63 2017 (print) Ɏ LCC BV85 (ebook) Ɏ DDC
242/.34--dc23
LC record available at https://lccn.loc.gov/2016041478

Paperback ISBN: 978-0-8024-3273-5

Originally delivered by fleets of horse-drawn wagons, the affordable paperbacks from D. L. Moody's publishing house resourced the church and served everyday people. Now, after more than 125 years of publishing and ministry, Moody Publishers' mission remains the same—even if our delivery systems have changed a bit. For more information on other books (and resources) created from a biblical perspective, go to www.moodypublishers.com or write to:

Moody Publishers
820 N. LaSalle Boulevard
Chicago, IL 60610

1 3 5 7 9 10 8 6 4 2

Printed in the United States of America

CONTENTS

A JOURNEY FROM DEATH TO NEW LIFE

From the Grave is a collection of forty daily readings from the beloved twentieth-century pastor and writer A. W. Tozer (1897–1963). The selections have been gleaned from his recorded sermons—which have been edited for print—his published books, and his editorials while serving as editor of *The Alliance Witness* magazine (now *Alliance Life*). Each reflection has been carefully selected for the season of Lent.

Lent is the time of waiting and preparing for Easter. Stemming from the Old English term *lent(c)ten*, Lent simply means "spring season," yet it refers to the Latin term *Quadragesima*, which means "fortieth." The forty days of Lent, which begins on Ash Wednesday and ends with the Saturday before Easter Sunday, commemorate Jesus' forty days in the wilderness, when He fasted and was tempted by the devil. The purpose of the season of Lent, therefore, is to prepare believers for commemorating Jesus' self-sacrifice, especially as it is displayed in His death and resurrection, and to help them experience in a concrete way the Christian journey from death to new life.

Common practices associated with Lent include fasting, self-examination and repentance, acts of self-denial, extended times of prayer, following prescribed Scripture readings and prayers, and reading daily devotionals. This devotional was compiled to help readers grow in their faith by reflecting on Christ's self-sacrificial love, His passion and death, His victory over sin and the grave, and what all this means for our lives as Christians.

For each day, you will find one or more passages of Scripture included with each excerpt from Tozer. The editors of this volume suggest that the reader contemplate each devotional throughout the day and how it unpacks the truth of Scripture. Traditionally, the forty days of Lent do not include Sundays, which are considered "Feast Days" in certain traditions. On these days, readers are welcome to reflect either on previous devotionals or on passages of Scripture not included in this volume.

As a result of reading these devotional selections, Tozer would want readers not simply to learn more about God's work in Christ, but truly to offer themselves as living sacrifices to God and worship Him in awe and gratitude.

—THE EDITORS

Week 1

THE HUNGER OF THE WILDERNESS

Blessed are the pure in heart, for they will see God.

MATTHEW 5:8

Every farmer knows the hunger of the wilderness—
that hunger which no modern farm machinery, no
improved agricultural methods, can ever quite destroy.
No matter how well prepared the soil, how well kept the
fences, how carefully painted the buildings, let the owner
neglect for a while his prized and valued acres and they
will revert again to the wild and be swallowed up by the
jungle or the wasteland. The bias of nature is toward
the wilderness, never toward the fruitful field. That, we
repeat, every farmer knows.

To the alert Christian this fact will be more than an

observation of interest to farmers; it will be a parable, an object lesson setting forth a law that runs through all the regions of our fallen world, affecting things spiritual as well as things material. We cannot escape the law that would persuade all things to remain wild or to return to a wild state after a period of cultivation. What is true of the field is true also of the soul, if we are but wise enough to see it.

The moral bent of the fallen world is not toward godliness, but definitely away from it. "Is this vile world a friend to grace," asks the poet rhetorically, "to help me on to God?" The sad answer is *no*, and it would be well for us to see that each new Christian learn this lesson as soon as possible after his conversion. We sometimes leave the impression that it is possible to find at an altar of prayer, once and for all, purity of heart and power to assure victorious living for the rest of our days. How wrong this notion is has been proved by countless numbers of Christians through the centuries.

The truth is that no spiritual experience, however revolutionary, can exempt us from temptation; and what is temptation but the effort of the wilderness to encroach upon our new-cleared field? The purified heart is obnoxious to the devil and to all the forces of the lost world. They will not rest until they have won back what they have lost. The jungle will creep in and seek to swallow up the tiny areas that have been made free by the power of the Holy Ghost. Only watchfulness and constant prayer can preserve those moral gains won for us through the operations of God's grace.

The neglected heart will soon be a heart overrun with worldly thoughts. The neglected life will soon become a moral chaos. The church that is not jealously protected by mighty intercession and sacrificial labors will before long become the abode of every evil bird and the hiding place for unsuspected corruption. The creeping wilderness will soon take over that church that trusts in its own strength and forgets to watch and pray.

FAITH IS A PERTURBING THING

For in Christ Jesus neither circumcision nor uncircumcision has any value. The only thing that counts is faith expressing itself through love.

GALATIANS 5:6

The faith of Paul and Luther was a revolutionizing thing. It upset the whole life of the individual and made him into another person altogether. It laid hold on the life and brought it under obedience to Christ. It took up its cross and followed along after Jesus with no intention of going back. It said goodbye to its old friends as certainly as Elijah when he stepped into the fiery chariot and went away in the whirlwind. It had a finality about it. It snapped shut on a man's heart like a trap; it captured the man and made him from that moment forward a happy love-servant of his Lord. It turned earth into a desert and drew heaven within sight of the believing soul. It realigned all life's actions and brought them into accord with the will of God. It set its possessor on a pinnacle of truth from which spiritual vantage point he viewed everything that came into his field of experience. It made him little and God big and Christ unspeakably dear. All this and more happened to a man when he received the faith that justifies.

Came the revolution, quietly, certainly, and put another construction upon the word *faith*. Little by little the whole meaning of the word shifted from what it had been to what it is now. And so insidious was the change that hardly a voice has been raised to warn against it. But the tragic consequences are all around us.

Faith now means no more than passive moral acquiescence in the Word of God and the cross of Jesus. To exercise it we have only to rest on one knee and nod our heads in agreement with the instructions of a personal worker intent upon saving our soul. The general effect is much the same as that which men feel after a visit to a good and wise doctor. They come back from such a visit feeling extra good, withal smiling just a little sheepishly to think how many fears they had entertained about their health when actually there was nothing wrong with them. They just needed rest.

Such a faith as this does not perturb people. It

comforts them. It does not put their hip out of joint so that they halt upon their thigh; rather it teaches them deep breathing exercises and improves their posture. The face of their ego is washed and their self-confidence is rescued from discouragement. All this they gain, but they do not get a new name as Jacob did, nor do they limp into the eternal sunlight. "As he passed over Penuel the sun rose upon him" (Genesis 32:31). That was Jacob—rather, that was Israel, for the sun did not shine much upon Jacob. It was ashamed to. But it loved to rest upon the head of the man who God had transformed.

This generation of Christians must hear again the doctrine of the perturbing quality of faith.

People must be told that the Christian religion is not something they can trifle with. The faith of Christ will command or it will have nothing to do with a man. It will not yield to experimentation. Its power cannot reach any man who is secretly keeping an escape route open in case things get too tough for him. The only man who can be sure he has true Bible faith is the one who has put himself in a position where he cannot go back. His faith has resulted in an everlasting and irrevocable committal, and however strongly he may be tempted he always replies, "Lord, to whom shall we go? thou hast the words of eternal life" (John 6:68).

THE USES OF SUFFERING

. . . we also glory in our sufferings, because we know that suffering produces perseverance; perseverance, character; and character, hope. And hope does not put us to shame, because God's love has been poured out into our hearts through the Holy Spirit, who has been given to us.

ROMANS 5:3–5

The Bible has a great deal to say about suffering, and most of it is encouraging. The prevailing religious mood is not favorable to the doctrine, but anything that gets as much space as the doctrine of suffering gets in the Scriptures should certainly receive careful and reverent attention from the sons of the new creation. We cannot afford to neglect it, for whether we understand it or not we are going to experience some suffering. As human beings we cannot escape it.

From the first cold shock that brings a howl of protest from the newborn infant down to the last anguished gasp of the aged man, pain and suffering dog our footsteps as we journey here below. It will pay us to learn what God says about it so that we may know how to act and what to expect when it comes.

Christianity embraces everything that touches the life of man and deals with it all effectively. Because suffering is a real part of human life, Christ Himself took part in the same and learned obedience by the things which He suffered. It is not possible that the afflicted saint should feel a stab of pain to which Christ is a stranger. Our Lord not only suffered once on earth, He suffers now along with His people. "Behold," cried the old saint as he watched a youthful martyr die, "Behold how our Lord suffers in the body of His handmaid."

> Think not thou canst sigh a sigh
> And thy Maker is not by;
> Think not thou canst weep a tear
> And thy Maker is not near.

There is a kind of suffering which profits no one: it is the bitter and defiant suffering of the lost. The man out of Christ may endure any degree of affliction without being any the wiser or the better for it. It is for him all a part of the tragic heritage of sin, a kind of earnest of the pains of hell. To such there is not much that we can say and for such there is little that we can do except to try in the name of Christ and our common humanity to reduce the suffering as much as we can. That much we owe to all the children of misfortune, whatever their color or race or creed.

As long as we remain in the body we shall be subject to a certain amount of that common suffering which we must share with all the sons of men—loss, bereavement, nameless heartaches, disappointments, partings, betrayals, and griefs of a thousand sorts. This is the less profitable kind of suffering, but even this can be made to serve the followers of Christ. There is such a thing as consecrated griefs, sorrows that may be common to everyone but which take on a special character for the Christian when accepted intelligently and offered to God in loving submission. We should be watchful lest we lose any blessing which such suffering might bring.

But there is another kind of suffering, known only to the Christian: it is voluntary suffering deliberately and knowingly incurred for the sake of Christ. Such is a luxury, a treasure of fabulous value, a source of riches beyond the power of the mind to conceive. And it is rare as well as precious, for there are few in this decadent age who will of their own choice go down into this dark mine looking for jewels. But of our own choice it must be, for there is no other way to get down. God will not force us into this kind of suffering; He will not lay this cross upon us nor embarrass us with riches we do not want. Such riches are reserved for those who apply to serve in the legion unto the death, who volunteer to suffer for Christ's sake and who follow up their application with lives that challenge the devil and invite the fury of hell. Such as these have said goodbye to the world's toys; they have chosen to suffer affliction with the people of God; they have accepted toil and suffering as their earthly portion. The marks of the cross are upon them, and they are known in heaven and hell.

DAY 4

TAKING TIME TO KNOW GOD

Keep this Book of the Law always on your lips; meditate on it day and night, so that you may be careful to do everything written in it. Then you will be prosperous and successful.

JOSHUA 1:8

Probably the most widespread and persistent problem to be found among Christians is the problem of retarded spiritual progress. Why, after years of Christian profession, do so many persons find themselves no further along than when they first believed?

Some would try to resolve the difficulty by asserting flatly that such persons were never saved, that they have never been truly regenerated. They are simply deceived professors who have stopped short of true conversion.

With a few this may be the answer, and we would accept this explanation as final did we not know that it is never the deceived professor who laments his lack of spiritual growth, but the true Christian who has had a real experience of conversion and who is sure that he is this very moment trusting in Christ for salvation. Uncounted numbers of such believers are among the disappointed ones who deplore their failure to make progress in the spiritual life.

The causes of retarded growth are many. It would not be accurate to ascribe the trouble to one single fault. One there is, however, which is so universal that it may easily be the main cause: *failure to give time to the cultivation of the knowledge of God.*

The temptation to make our relation to God judicial instead of personal is very strong. Believing for salvation has these days been reduced to a once-done act that requires no further attention. The young believer becomes aware of a living Savior to be followed and adored.

The Christian is strong or weak depending upon how closely he has cultivated the knowledge of God. Paul was anything but an advocate of the once-done, automatic school of Christianity. He devoted his whole life to the art of knowing Christ.

> Yea doubtless, and I count all things but loss
> for the excellency of the knowledge of Christ

Jesus my Lord: for whom I have suffered the loss of all things, and do count them but dung, that I may win Christ. . . . That I may know him, and the power of his resurrection, and the fellowship of his sufferings, being made conformable unto his death. . . . I press toward the mark for the prize of the high calling of God in Christ Jesus. (Philippians 3:8, 10, 14)

Progress in the Christian life is exactly equal to the growing knowledge we gain of the triune God in personal experience. And such experience requires a whole life devoted to it and plenty of time spent at the holy task of cultivating God. God can be known satisfactorily only as we devote time to Him. Without meaning to do it we have written our serious fault into our book titles and gospel songs. "A little talk with Jesus," we sing, and call our books *God's Minute*, or something else as revealing. The Christian who is satisfied to give God His "minute" and to "have a little talk with Jesus" is the same one who shows up at the evangelistic service weeping over his retarded spiritual growth and begging the evangelist to show him the way out of his difficulty.

A thousand distractions would woo us away from thoughts of God, but if we are wise we will sternly put them from us and make room for the King and take time to entertain Him. Some things may be neglected with but little loss to the spiritual life, but to neglect communion with God is to hurt ourselves where we cannot afford it. God will respond to our efforts to know Him. The Bible tells us how; it is altogether a matter of how much determination we bring to the holy task.

Week 2

NO REGENERATION WITHOUT REFORMATION

Produce fruit in keeping with repentance.

MATTHEW 3:8

I n the Bible, the offer of pardon on the part of God is conditioned upon intention to reform on the part of man. There can be no spiritual regeneration till there has been moral reformation. That this statement requires defense only proves how far from the truth we have strayed.

In our current popular theology pardon depends upon faith alone. The very word *reform* has been banished from among the sons of the Reformation!

We often hear the declaration, "I do not preach reformation; I preach regeneration." Now we recognize this as
being the expression of a commendable revolt against the
insipid and unscriptural doctrine of salvation by human
effort. But the declaration as it stands contains real error,
for it opposes reformation to regeneration. Actually, the
two are never opposed to each other in sound Bible theology. The not-reformation-but-regeneration doctrine
incorrectly presents us with an either-or; either you take
reformation or you take regeneration. This is inaccurate.
The fact is that on this subject we are presented not with
an either-or, but with both-and. The converted man is
both reformed and regenerated. And unless the sinner
is willing to reform his way of living, he will never know
the inward experience of regeneration. This is vital truth
which has gotten lost under the leaves in popular evangelical theology.

The idea that God will pardon a rebel who has not
given up his rebellion is contrary both to the Scriptures
and to common sense. How horrible to contemplate a
church full of persons who have been pardoned but who
still love sin and hate the ways of righteousness. And
how much more horrible to think of heaven as filled with
sinners who had not repented nor changed their ways of
living.

A familiar story will illustrate this. The governor of
one of our states was visiting the state prison incognito.
He fell into conversation with a personable young convict

and felt a secret wish to pardon him. "What would you do," he asked casually, "if you were lucky enough to obtain a pardon?" The convict, not knowing to whom he was speaking, snarled his reply: "If I ever get out of this place, the first thing I'll do is cut the throat of the judge who sent me here." The governor broke off the conversation and withdrew from the cell. The convict stayed on in prison. To pardon a man who had not reformed would be to let loose another killer upon society. That kind of pardon would not only be foolish, it would be downright immoral.

The promise of pardon and cleansing is always associated in the Scriptures with the command to repent. The widely used text in Isaiah, "Though your sins be as scarlet, they shall be as white as snow; though they be red like crimson, they shall be as wool" (Isaiah 1:18), is organically united to the verses that precede it: "Wash you, make you clean; put away the evil of your doings from before mine eyes; cease to do evil; learn to do well; seek judgment, relieve the oppressed, judge the fatherless, plead for the widow" (1:16–17). What does this teach but radical reformation of life before there can be any expectation of pardon? To divorce the words from each other is to do violence to the Scriptures and to convict ourselves of deceitfully handling the truth.

I think there is little doubt that the teaching of salvation without repentance has lowered the moral standards of the Church and produced a multitude of deceived religious professors who erroneously believe themselves to be saved when in fact they are still in the gall of bitterness and the bond of iniquity. And to see such persons actually seeking the deeper life is a grim and disillusioning sight. Yet our altars are sometimes filled with seekers who are crying with Simon, "Give me this power," when the moral groundwork has simply not been laid for it. The whole thing must be acknowledged as a clear victory for the devil, a victory he could never have enjoyed if unwise teachers had not made it possible by preaching the evil doctrine of regeneration apart from reformation.

BE HOLY!

*But just as he who called you is holy, so be holy in all
you do; for it is written: "Be holy, because I am holy."*

1 PETER 1:15–16

Y ou cannot study the Bible diligently and earnestly
without being struck by an obvious fact: the whole
matter of personal holiness is highly important to God!

Neither do you have to give long study to the attitudes
of modern Christian believers to discern that by and large
we consider the expression of true Christian holiness to
be just a matter of personal option: "I have looked it over
and considered it, but I don't buy it!"

I have always liked the word *exhort* better than *command*,
so I remind you that Peter has given every Christian a
forceful exhortation to holiness of life and conversation.
He clearly bases this exhortation on two great facts: first,

the character of God, and second, the command of God.

His argument comes out so simply that we sophisticates stumble over it: God's children ought to be holy because God Himself is holy! We so easily overlook the fact that Peter was an apostle, and he is here confronting us with the force of an apostolic injunction, completely in line with the Old Testament truth concerning the person and character of God, and also in line with what the Lord Jesus had taught and revealed to His disciples and followers.

Personally, I am of the opinion that we who claim to be apostolic Christians do not have the privilege of ignoring such apostolic injunctions. I do not mean that a pastor can forbid or that a church can compel. I mean only that morally we dare not ignore this commandment, "Be ye holy."

Because it is an apostolic word, we must face up to the fact that we will have to deal with it in some way, and not ignore it—as some Christians do. Certainly no one has provided us with an option in this matter. Who has ever given us the right or the privilege to look into the Bible and say, "I am willing to consider this matter and if I like it, I will buy it"—using the language of the day? There is something basically wrong with our Christianity and our spirituality if we can carelessly presume that if we do not like a biblical doctrine and choose not to "buy" it, there is no harm done.

Commandments which we have received from our Lord or from the apostles cannot be overlooked or ignored by earnest and committed Christians. God has never instructed us that we should weigh His desires for us and His commandments to us in the balances of our own judgment and then decide what we want to do about them.

A professing Christian may say, "I have found a place of real Christian freedom; these things just don't apply to me."

Of course you can walk out on it! God has given every one of us the power to make our own choices. I am not saying that we are forced to bow our necks to this yoke and we do not have to apply it to ourselves. It is true that if we do not like it, we can turn our backs on it.

The record in the New Testament is plain on this point—many people followed Jesus for a while and then walked away from Him. Once Jesus said to His disciples: "Except ye eat my body, my flesh, and drink my blood, there is no life in you." Many looked at one another and then walked away from Him. Jesus turned to those remaining and said, "Will you also go away?" Peter gave the answer which is still my answer today: "Lord, if we wanted to go away, where would we go? Thou alone hast the words of eternal life."

Those were wise words, indeed, words born of love and devotion.

So, we are not forced to obey in the Christian life, but we are forced to make a choice at many points in our spiritual maturity.

We have that power within us to reject God's instructions—but where else shall we go?

BIBLE TAUGHT OR SPIRIT TAUGHT?

I pray that the eyes of your heart may be enlightened . . .
EPHESIANS 1:18

Most of us are acquainted with churches that teach the Bible to their children from their tenderest years, give them long instruction in the catechism, drill them further in pastor's classes and still never produce in them a living Christianity nor a virile godliness. Their members show no evidence of having passed from death unto life. None of the earmarks of salvation so plainly indicated in the Scriptures are found among them.

Their religious lives are correct and reasonably moral, but wholly mechanical and altogether lacking in radiance. They wear their faith as persons in mourning once wore black armbands to show their love and respect for the departed.

Such persons cannot be dismissed as hypocrites. Many of them are pathetically serious about it all. They are simply blind. From lack of the vital Spirit they are forced to get along with the outward shell of faith, while all the time their deep hearts are starving for spiritual reality and they do not know what is wrong with them.

This difference between the religion of creed and the religion of the Spirit is well set forth by the saintly Thomas in a tender little prayer to his Lord:

> The children of Israel in time past said unto Moses, "Speak thou with us, and we will hear: but let not God speak with us, lest we die." Not so, Lord, not so, I beseech Thee; but rather with the prophet Samuel I humbly and earnestly entreat, "Speak, Lord; for Thy servant heareth." Let not Moses speak unto me, nor any of the prophets, but rather do Thou speak, O Lord GOD, the inspirer, enlightener of all the prophets; for Thou alone without them canst perfectly instruct me, but they without Thee can profit nothing. They indeed may utter words, but they cannot give the Spirit. Most beautifully do they speak, but if Thou be silent, they inflame not the heart. They teach

the letter, but Thou openest the sense; they
bring forth mysteries, but Thou unlockest the
heart. . . . They cry aloud with words, but Thou
impartest understanding to the hearing.

It would be hard to wrap it up better than that. The
same thing has been said variously by others; however, the
most familiar saying probably is, "The Scriptures, to be
understood, must be read with the same Spirit that originally inspired them." No one denies this, but even such
a statement will go over the heads of those who hear it
unless the Holy Spirit inflames the heart.

The charge often made against us by liberals, that we
are "bibliolaters," is probably not true in the same sense
as meant by our detractors; but candor and self-analysis
will force us to admit that there is often too much truth
in their charge. Among religious persons of unquestioned
orthodoxy there is sometimes found a dull dependence
upon the letter of the text without the faintest understanding of its spirit. That truth is in its essence spiritual
must constantly be kept before our minds if we would
know the truth indeed. Jesus Christ is Himself the Truth,
and He cannot be confined to mere words even though,
as we ardently believe, He has Himself inspired the
words. That which is spiritual cannot be shut in by ink
or fenced in by type and paper. The best a book can do
is give us the letter of truth. If we ever receive more than
this, it must be by the Holy Spirit who gives it.

The great need of the hour among persons spiritually hungry is twofold: first, to know the Scriptures, apart from which no saving truth will be vouchsafed by our Lord; the second, to be enlightened by the Spirit, apart from whom the Scriptures will not be understood.

GOD IS EASY TO LIVE WITH

As a father has compassion on his children,
so the Lord has compassion on those who
fear him; for he knows how we are formed,
he remembers that we are dust.

PSALM 103:13–14

From a failure properly to understand God comes a world of unhappiness among good Christians even today. The Christian life is thought to be a glum, unrelieved cross-carrying under the eye of a stern Father who expects much and excuses nothing. He is austere, peevish, highly temperamental and extremely hard to please. The kind of life which springs out of such libelous notions must of necessity be but a parody on the true life in Christ.

It is most important to our spiritual welfare that we hold in our minds always a right conception of God. If we think of Him as cold and exacting, we shall find it impossible to love Him, and our lives will be ridden with servile fear. If, again, we hold Him to be kind and understanding, our whole inner life will mirror that idea.

The truth is that God is the most winsome of all beings and His service one of unspeakable pleasure. He is all love, and those who trust Him need never know anything but that love. He is just indeed and He will not condone sin; but through the blood of the everlasting covenant He is able to act toward us exactly as if we had never sinned. Toward the trusting sons of men His mercy will always triumph over justice.

The fellowship of God is delightful beyond all telling. He communes with His redeemed ones in an easy, uninhibited fellowship that is restful and healing to the soul. He is not sensitive or selfish nor temperamental. What He is today we shall find Him tomorrow and the next day and the next year. He is not hard to please, though He may be hard to satisfy. He expects of us only what He has Himself first supplied. He is quick to mark every simple effort to please Him, and just as quick to overlook imperfections when He knows we meant to do His will. He loves us for ourselves and values our love more than galaxies of new created worlds.

Unfortunately, many Christians cannot get free from their perverted notions of God, and these notions poison their hearts and destroy their inward freedom. These friends serve God grimly, as the elder brother did, doing what is right without enthusiasm and without joy, and seem altogether unable to understand the buoyant, spirited celebration when the prodigal comes home. Their idea of God rules out the possibility of His being happy in His people, and they attribute the singing and shouting to sheer fanaticism. Unhappy souls, these, doomed to go heavily on their melancholy way, grimly determined to do right if the heavens fall and to be on the winning side in the day of judgment.

How good it would be if we could learn that God is easy to live with. He remembers our frame and knows that we are dust. He may sometimes chasten us, it is true, but even this He does with a smile, the proud, tender smile of a Father who is bursting with pleasure over an imperfect but promising son who is coming every day to look more and more like the One whose child he is.

Some of us are religiously jumpy and self-conscious because we know that God sees our every thought and is acquainted with all our ways. We need not be. God is the sum of all patience and the essence of kindly good will. We please Him most, not by frantically trying to make ourselves good, but by throwing ourselves into His arms with all our imperfections, and believing that He understands everything and loves us still.

TRUE FAITH BRINGS COMMITMENT

Many claim to have unfailing love,
but a faithful person who can find?

PROVERBS 20:6

To many Christians, Christ is little more than an idea, or at best an ideal; He is not a fact. Millions of professed believers talk as if He were real but act as if He were not. And always our actual position is to be discovered by the way we act, not by the way we talk.

We can prove our faith by our committal to it and in no other way. Any belief that does not command the one who holds it is not a real belief; it is a pseudo belief only. And it might shock some of us profoundly if we were brought suddenly face-to-face with our beliefs and forced to test them in the fires of practical living.

Many of us Christians have become extremely skillful in arranging our lives so as to admit the truth of Christianity without being embarrassed by its implications. We arrange things so that we can get on well enough without divine aid, while at the same time ostensibly seeking it. We boast in the Lord but watch carefully that we never get caught depending on Him. "The heart is deceitful above all things, and desperately wicked: who can know it?" (Jeremiah 17:9).

Pseudo faith always arranges a way out to serve in case God fails it. Real faith knows only one way and gladly allows itself to be stripped of any second way or makeshift substitutes. For true faith, it is either God or total collapse. And not since Adam first stood up on the earth has God failed a single man or woman who trusted Him.

The man of pseudo faith will fight for his verbal creed but refuse flatly to allow himself to get into a predicament where his future must depend upon that creed being true. He always provides himself with secondary ways of escape so he will have a way out if the roof caves in.

What we need very badly these days is a company of Christians who are prepared to trust God as completely now as they know they must do at the last day. For each of us the time is surely coming when we shall have nothing but God. Health and wealth and friends and hiding places will all be swept away and we shall have only God. To the man of pseudo faith that is a terrifying thought, but to real faith it is one of the most comforting thoughts the heart can entertain.

It would be a tragedy indeed to come to the place where we have no other but God and find that we had not really been trusting God during the days of our earthly sojourn. It would be better to invite God now to remove every false trust, to disengage our hearts from all secret hiding places and to bring us out into the open where we can discover for ourselves whether or not we actually trust Him. That is a harsh cure for our troubles, but it is a sure one. Gentler cures may be too weak to do the work. And time is running out on us.

THE KEY TO SPIRITUAL POWER

Whoever wants to be my disciple must deny themselves and take up their cross and follow me.

MATTHEW 16:24

S ome people in reading the Bible say they cannot under-stand why Elijah and other men had such active power with the living God. It is quite simple. God heard Elijah because Elijah had heard God. God did according to the word of Elijah because Elijah had done according to the word of God. You cannot separate the two.

When we are willing to consider the active will of God for our lives, we come immediately to a personal knowl-edge of the cross because the will of God is the place of blessed, painful, fruitful trouble! The Apostle Paul knew

about that. He called it "the fellowship of Christ's sufferings." It is my conviction that one of the reasons we
exhibit very little spiritual power is because we are unwilling to accept and experience the fellowship of the Savior's
sufferings, which means acceptance of His cross.

How can we have and know the blessed intimacy of the
Lord Jesus if we are unwilling to take the route which He
has demonstrated? We do not have it because we refuse
to relate the will of God to the cross.

All of the great saints have been acquainted with the
cross—even those who lived before the time of Christ.
They were acquainted with the cross in essence because
their obedience brought it to them. All Christians living
in full obedience will experience the cross and find themselves exercised in spirit very frequently. If they know
their own hearts, they will be prepared to wrestle with the
cross when it comes.

Think of Jacob in the Old Testament and notice the
direction from which his cross came—directly from his
own carnal self. It took Jacob some time to discover the
nature of his own heart and to admit and confess that
Jacob's cross was Jacob himself.

Read again about Daniel and you will discover that his
cross was the world. Consider Job and you will find that
his cross was the devil. The devil crucified Job, the world
crucified Daniel, and Jacob was crucified on the tree of
his own Jacobness, his own carnality.

Study the lives of the apostles in the New Testament and you will find that their crosses came from the religious authorities.

Likewise in Church history we look at Luther and note that his cross came from the Roman Church which makes so much of wooden crosses, while Wesley's cross came from the Protestant Church. Continue to name the great souls who followed the will of God, and you will name the men and women of God who looked forward by faith, and their obedience invariably led them into places of blessed and painful and fruitful trouble.

I must point out here the fallacy of thinking that in following Jesus we can easily go up on the hillside and die—just like that! I admit that when Jesus was here on earth, the easiest and cheapest way to get off was to follow Jesus physically. Anyone could get out of work and say goodbye with the explanation, "I am going to follow Jesus." Multitudes did this. They followed Him physically, but they had no understanding of Him spiritually. Therefore, in that day the cheapest, easiest way to dispose of the cross was to carry it physically.

But brethren, taking our cross is not going to mean the physical act of following Jesus along a dusty pathway. We are not going to climb the hill where there are already two crosses in place and be nailed up between them.

Our cross will be determined by whatever pain and suffering and trouble which will yet come to us because of

our obedience to the will of God. The true saints of God
have always borne witness that wholehearted obedience
brings the cross into the light quicker than anything else.

Week 3

THE TERROR
OF THE LORD

*Do not be afraid of those who kill the body but
cannot kill the soul. Rather, be afraid of the
One who can destroy both soul and body in hell.*

MATTHEW 10:28

We have but to read the Scriptures with our eyes open and we can see this truth running like a strong cable from Genesis to Revelation: the presence of the divine always brought fear to the hearts of sinful men. Always there was about any manifestation of God something that dismayed the onlookers, that daunted and overawed them, that struck them with a terror more than natural. This terror had no relation to mere fear of bodily harm. It was a dread consternation experienced far in toward the center and core of the nature, much farther in than that fear experienced as a normal result of the instinct for physical self-preservation.

I do not believe that any lasting good can come from religious activities that do not root in this quality of creature-fear. The animal in us is very strong and altogether self-confident. Until it has been defeated God will not show Himself to the eyes of our faith. Until we have been gripped by that nameless terror which results when an unholy creature is suddenly confronted by that One who is the holiest of all, we are not likely to be much affected by the doctrine of love and grace as it is declared by the New Testament evangel. The love of God affects a carnal heart not at all; or if at all, then adversely, for the knowledge that God loves us may simply confirm us in our self-righteousness.

The effort of liberal and borderline modernists to woo men to God by presenting the soft side of religion is an unqualified evil because it ignores the very reason for our alienation from God in the first place. Until a man has gotten into trouble with his heart he is not likely to get out of trouble with God. Cain and Abel are two solemn examples of this truth. Cain brought a present to One whom he assumed to be pleased with him. Abel brought a sacrifice to One whom he knew could not accept him as he was. His trembling heart told him to find a place to hide. Cain's heart did not tremble. Cain was well satisfied with himself, so he sought no hiding place. The fear of

God would have served Cain well in that critical moment, for it would have changed the whole character of his offering and altered the entire course of his life for the better.

As indispensable as is the terror of the Lord, we must always keep in mind that it cannot be induced by threats made in the name of the Lord. Hell and judgment are realities, and they must be preached in their biblical context as fully as the Bible teaches them, no more and no less; but they cannot induce that mysterious thing we call the fear of the Lord. Such fear is a supernatural thing, having no relation to threats of punishment. It has about it a mysterious quality, often without much intellectual content; it is a feeling rather than an idea; it is the deep reaction of a fallen creature in the presence of the holy Being the stunned heart knows is God. The Holy Spirit alone can induce this emotion in the human breast. All effort on our part to superinduce it is wasted, or worse.

OUR ENEMY CONTENTMENT

*I know what it is to be in need, and I know what it is
to have plenty. I have learned the secret of being
content in any and every situation, whether well
fed or hungry, whether living in plenty or in want.*

PHILIPPIANS 4:12

Contentment with earthly goods is the mark of a saint; contentment with our spiritual state is a mark of inward blindness.

One of the greatest fears of the Christian is religious complacency. The man who believes he has arrived will not go any farther; from his standpoint it would be foolish to do so. The snare is to believe we have arrived when we have not. The present neat habit of quoting a text to prove we have arrived may be a dangerous one if in truth we have no actual inward experience of the text. Truth that is not experienced is no better than error and may be fully as dangerous. The scribes who sat in Moses's seat were not the victims of error; they were the victims of their failure to experience the truth they taught.

Religious complacency is encountered almost everywhere among Christians these days, and its presence is a sign and a prophecy. For every Christian will become at last what his desires have made him. We are all the sum total of our hungers. The great saints have all had thirsting hearts. Their cry has been, "My soul thirsteth for God, for the living God: when shall I come and appear before God?" (Psalm 42:2). Their longing after God all but consumed them; it propelled them onward and upward to heights toward which less ardent Christians look with languid eye and entertain no hope of reaching.

Orthodox Christianity has fallen to its present low estate from lack of spiritual desire. Among the many who profess the Christian faith, scarcely one in a thousand reveals any passionate thirst for God. The practice of many of our spiritual advisers is to use the Scriptures to discourage such little longing as may be discovered here and there among us. We fear extremes and shy away from too much ardor in religion as if it were possible to have too much love or too much faith or too much holiness.

Occasionally one's heart is cheered by the discovery of some insatiable saint who is willing to sacrifice everything for the sheer joy of experiencing God in increasing intimacy. To such we offer this word of exhortation: pray on, fight on, sing on. Do not underrate anything God may have done for you heretofore. Thank God for everything up to this point, but do not stop here. Press on into the deep things of God. Insist upon tasting the profounder mysteries of redemption. Keep your feet on the ground, but let your heart soar as high as it will. Refuse to be average or to surrender to the chill of your spiritual environment. If you thus "follow after," heaven will surely be opened to you and you will, with Ezekiel, see visions of God.

Unless you do these things you will reach at last (and unknown to you) the boneyard of orthodoxy and be doomed to live out your days in a spiritual state which can be best described as "the dead level and quintessence of every mediocrity." From such a state God save us all.

STOPPED DEAD IN YOUR TRACKS?

I press on toward the goal to win the prize for which God has called me heavenward in Christ Jesus.

PHILIPPIANS 3:14

I blame faulty exposition of the New Testament for stopping many Christians dead in their tracks, causing them to shrug off any suggestion that there is still spiritual advance and progress beckoning them on.

The position of some would-be teachers which insists that when you come into the kingdom of God by faith you immediately have all there is in the kingdom of God is as deadly as cyanide. It kills all hope of spiritual advance and causes many to adopt what I call "the creed of contentment."

Why should a Christian settle down as soon as he has come to know the Lord?

I would have to reply that he must have received faulty counsel and bad exposition of New Testament truth. There is always real joy in the heart of the person who has become a child of God, and proper and sound teaching of the Word of God will awake desire within him to move forward in spiritual adventure with Christ.

But the would-be teacher may tell the new Christian, "You are now complete in Him. The Bible says that and it means that you should just be glad that you are complete and there is nothing more you will ever need!" From that time on any effort to forge ahead for God is put down as some sort of fanaticism. This kind of exposition has brought many Christians into a place of false contentment—satisfied to stay right where they are.

But not so with the Apostle Paul who amazes and humbles us as we read in the third chapter of Philippians of his earnest desire to press forward and to become a special kind of Christian.

With great desire, he wrote: "That I may gain Christ"—and yet he already had Christ!

With obvious longing he said, "That I may be found in Him"—and yet he was already in Him. We go to Paul more than to any other writer in the Bible to learn the doctrine of being in Christ and yet Paul humbly and intensely breathed this great desire, "I want to know Christ," when he already knew Him!

It was this same Paul who gladly testified, "I am crucified with Christ: nevertheless I live; yet not I, but Christ liveth in me: and the life which I now live in the flesh I live by the faith of the Son of God, who loved me, and gave himself for me" (Galatians 2:20).

Yet, because he could never be standing still, he further testified, "But I follow after, if that I may apprehend that for which also I am apprehended of Christ Jesus" (Philippians 3:12b).

How utterly foreign that is to the spirit of modern orthodoxy! How foreign to the bland assurances that because we can quote the text of Scripture we must have the experience. This strange textualism that assumes that because we can quote chapter and verse we possess the content and experience is a grave hindrance to spiritual progress. I think it is one of the deadliest, most chilling breezes that ever blew across the church of God!

Too many of us are complete strangers to the desire and the spirit which drove the Apostle Paul forward day by day. "That I may gain—that I may know—that I may be found in Him"—these were the words that drove Paul. But now, we are often told that we "have" everything, and that we should just be thankful and "go on to cultivate." I say that the two attitudes are foreign to one another. They do not belong together.

We are told to study the biblical passages in the Greek. We find out what they mean in English. Then we say, "Well, isn't that fine—isn't that fine!" And that is all we do about it. But Paul said, "I press toward the mark for the prize of the high calling of God in Christ Jesus" (Philippians 3:14).

CODDLED OR CRUCIFIED?

. . . those of you who do not give up
everything you have cannot be my disciples.

LUKE 14:33

The spiritual giants of old would not take their religion the easy way nor offer unto God that which cost them nothing. They sought not comfort but holiness, and the pages of history are still wet with their blood and their tears.

We now live in softer times. Woe unto us, for we have become adept in the art of comforting ourselves without power.

Almost every radical effort of the Holy Spirit to lead us forth to heroic self-crucifixion is now tempered with a fine sophistry drawn from—of all sources—the Word of God itself. I hear it often these days. The trick is to say, half comically, amused at our own former ignorance, "Once I was distressed over my lack of power, my spiritual sterility, as I then thought; but one day the Lord said to me, 'My child, etc., etc.'" Then follows a quotation direct from the mouth of the Lord condoning our weakness and self-coddling. Thus the very authority of divine inspiration is given to what is obviously but the defensive reasoning of our own hearts.

Those who will justify themselves in that kind of dodging are not likely to be much affected by anything I can say or write. No one is so dead as the man who has turned the very thunders of judgment into a lullaby to soothe him into sound sleep and has made the sacred Scriptures themselves a hiding place from reality.

But to those who will hear I would say with all the urgency at my command: Though the cross of Christ has been beautified by the poet and the artist, the avid seeker after God is likely to find it the same savage implement of destruction it was in the days of old. The way of the cross is still the pain-wracked path to spiritual power and fruitfulness.

So do not seek to hide from it. Do not accept an easy way. Do not allow yourself to be patted to sleep in a comfortable church, void of power and barren of fruit. Do not paint the cross nor deck it with flowers. Take it for what it is, as it is, and you will find it the rugged way to death and life. Let it slay you utterly. Seek God. Seek to be holy and fear none of those things which you will suffer.

THE GREAT DISPARITY

Watch your life and doctrine closely.
Persevere in them, because if you do, you
will save both yourself and your hearers.

1 TIMOTHY 4:16

There is an evil which I have seen under the sun and which in its effect upon the Christian religion may be more destructive than communism, Romanism, and liberalism combined. It is the glaring disparity between theology and practice among professing Christians.

So wide is the gulf that separates theory from practice in the Church that an inquiring stranger who chances upon both would scarcely dream that there was any relation between them. An intelligent observer of our human scene who heard the Sunday morning sermon and later watched the Sunday afternoon conduct of those who had heard it would conclude that he had been examining two distinct and contrary religions.

A church conference, for instance, may listen to and applaud the most spiritual message, and twenty minutes later adopt the most carnal procedure, altogether as if they had not heard the impassioned moral appeal a few moments before. Christians habitually weep and pray over beautiful truth, only to draw back from that same truth when it comes to the difficult job of putting it in practice. The average church simply does not dare to check its practices against biblical precepts. It tolerates things that are diametrically opposed to the will of God, and if the matter is pointed out to its leaders they will defend its unscriptural practices with a smooth casuistry equal to the verbal dodging of the Roman moralists.

This can be explained only by assuming a lack of integration in the religious personality. There seems to be no vital connection between the emotional and volitional departments of the life. The mind can approve and the emotions enjoy while the will drags its feet and refuses to go along. And since Christ makes His appeal directly to the will, are we not justified in wondering whether or not these divided souls have ever made a true committal to the Lord? Or whether they have been inwardly renewed?

It appears that too many Christians want to enjoy the thrill of feeling right but are not willing to endure the inconvenience of being right. So the divorce between theory and practice becomes permanent in fact, though in word the union is declared to be eternal. Truth sits forsaken and grieves till her professed followers come home for a brief visit, but she sees them depart again when the bills become due. They protest great and undying love for her but they will not let their love cost them anything.

Could this be the condition our Lord had in mind when He said, "Thou hast a name that thou livest, and art dead" (Revelation 3:1)? What can the effect be upon the spectators who live day after day among professed Christians who habitually ignore the commandments of Christ and live after their own private notions of Christianity? Will they not conclude that the whole thing is false? Will they not be forced to believe that the faith of Christ is an unreal and visionary thing which they are fully justified in rejecting?

Certainly the non-Christian is not too much to be blamed if he turns disgustedly away from the invitation of the gospel after he has been exposed for a while to the inconsistencies of those of his acquaintances who profess to follow Christ. The deadening effect of religious make-believe on the human mind is beyond all describing.

In that great and terrible day when the deeds of men are searched into by the penetrating eyes of the Judge of all the earth, what will we answer when we are charged with inconsistency and moral fraud? And at whose door will lie the blame for the millions of lost men who while they lived on earth were sickened and revolted by the religious travesty they knew as Christianity?

THE BLESSEDNESS OF POSSESSING NOTHING

Blessed are the poor in spirit,
for theirs is the kingdom of heaven.

MATTHEW 5:3

There is within the human heart a tough, fibrous root of fallen life whose nature is to possess, always to possess. It covets things with a deep and fierce passion. The pronouns *my* and *mine* look innocent enough in print, but their constant and universal uses are significant. They express the real nature of the old Adamic man better than a thousand volumes of theology could do. They are verbal symptoms of our deep disease. The roots of our hearts have grown down into things, and we dare not pull up one rootlet lest we die. Things have become necessary to us, a development never originally intended. God's gifts now take the place of God, and the whole course of nature is upset by the monstrous substitution.

Our Lord referred to this tyranny of things when He said to His disciples,

> If any man will come after me, let him deny
> himself, and take up his cross, and follow me.
> For whosoever will save his life shall lose it:
> and whosoever will lose his life for my sake
> shall find it.

MATTHEW 16:24–25

Breaking this truth into fragments for our better understanding, it would seem that there is within each of us an enemy which we tolerate at our peril. Jesus called it "life" and "self," or as we would say, the *self-life*. Its chief characteristic is its possessiveness; the words *gain* and *profit* suggest this. To allow this enemy to live is, in the end, to lose everything. To repudiate it and give up all for Christ's sake is to lose nothing at last, but to preserve everything unto life eternal. And possibly also a hint is given here as to the only effective way to destroy this foe: it is by the cross. "Let him take up his cross, and follow me" (see Matthew 16:24).

The way to deeper knowledge of God is through the lonely valleys of soul poverty and abnegation of all things. The blessed ones who possess the kingdom are they who have repudiated every external thing and have rooted from their hearts all sense of possessing. These are the "poor in spirit." They have reached an inward state paralleling the outward circumstances of the common beggar in the streets of Jerusalem. That is what the word *poor* as Christ used it actually means. These blessed poor are no longer slaves to the tyranny of things. They have broken the yoke of the oppressor; and this they have done not by fighting but by surrendering. Though free from all sense of possessing, they yet possess all things. "Theirs is the kingdom of heaven."

Let me exhort you to take this seriously. It is not to be understood as mere Bible teaching to be stored away in the mind along with an inert mass of other doctrines. It is a marker on the road to greener pastures, a path chiseled against the steep sides of the mount of God. We dare not try to bypass it if we would follow on in this holy pursuit. We must ascend a step at a time. If we refuse one step, we bring our progress to an end.

Week 4

NO ONE WANTS
TO DIE ON A CROSS

Whoever does not take up their
cross and follow me is not worthy of me.

MATTHEW 10:38

We are willing to join heartily in singing, "To God Be the Glory," but we are strangely ingenious in figuring out ways and means by which we keep some of the glory for ourselves. In this matter of perpetually seeking our own interests, we can only say that people who want to live for God often arrange to do very subtly what the worldly souls do crudely and openly.

A man who doesn't have enough imagination to invent anything will still figure out a way of seeking his own interests, and the amazing thing is that he will do it with the help of some pretext which will serve as a screen to keep him from seeing the ugliness of his own behavior.

Yes, we have it among professing Christians—this strange ingenuity to seek our own interest under the guise of seeking the interests of God. I am not afraid to say what I fear—that there are thousands of people who are using the deeper life and Bible prophecy, foreign missions and physical healing for no other purpose than to promote their own private interests secretly. They continue to let their apparent interest in these things serve as a screen so that they don't have to take a look at how ugly they are on the inside.

So we talk a lot about the deeper life and spiritual victory and becoming dead to ourselves—but we stay very busy rescuing ourselves from the cross. That part of ourselves that we rescue from the cross may be a very little part of us, but it is likely to be the seat of our spiritual troubles and our defeats.

No one wants to die on a cross—until he comes to the place where he is desperate for the highest will of God in serving Jesus Christ. The Apostle Paul said, "I want to die on that cross and I want to know what it is to die there, because if I die with Him I will also know Him in a better resurrection" (see Philippians 3:10–11). Paul was not just saying, "He will raise me from the dead"—for everyone will be raised from the dead. He said, "I want a superior resurrection, a resurrection like Christ's." Paul was willing to be crucified with Christ, but in our day we want to die a piece at a time, so we can rescue little parts of ourselves from the cross.

People will pray and ask God to be filled—but all the while there is that strange ingenuity, that contradiction within which prevents our wills from stirring to the point of letting God have His way.

Those who live in this state of perpetual contradiction cannot be happy Christians. A man who is always on the cross, just piece after piece, cannot be happy in that process. But when that man takes his place on the cross with Jesus Christ once and for all, and commends his spirit to God, lets go of everything and ceases to defend himself— sure, he has died, but there is a resurrection that follows!

If we are willing to go this route of victory with Jesus Christ, we cannot continue to be mediocre Christians, stopped halfway to the peak. Until we give up our own interests, there will never be enough stirring within our beings to find His highest will.

TRUE CULTIVATION

For God did not call us to be impure, but to live a holy life.

1 THESSALONIANS 4:7

The idea of cultivation and exercise, so dear to the saints of old, has now no place in our total religious picture. It is too slow, too common. We now demand glamour and fast-flowing dramatic action. A generation of Christians reared among push buttons and automatic machines is impatient of slower and less direct methods of reaching their goals. We have been trying to apply machine-age methods to our relations with God. We read our chapter, have our short devotions and rush away, hoping to make up for our deep inward bankruptcy by attending another gospel meeting or listening to another thrilling story told by a religious adventurer lately returned from afar.

The tragic results of this spirit are all about us: shallow lives, hollow religious philosophies, the preponderance of the element of fun in gospel meetings, the glorification of men, trust in religious externalities, quasi-religious fellowships, salesmanship methods, the mistaking of dynamic personality for the power of the Spirit. These and such as these are the symptoms of an evil disease, a deep and serious malady of the soul.

For this great sickness that is upon us no one person is responsible, and no Christian is wholly free from blame. We have all contributed, directly or indirectly, to this sad state of affairs. We have been too blind to see, or too timid to speak out, or too self-satisfied to desire anything better than the poor, average diet with which others appear satisfied. To put it differently, we have accepted one another's notions, copied one another's lives and made one another's experiences the model for our own. And for a generation the trend has been downward. Now we have reached a low place of sand and burnt wire grass and, worst of all, we have made the Word of Truth conform to our experience and accepted this low plane as the very pasture of the blessed.

It will require a determined heart and more than a little courage to wrench ourselves loose from the grip of our times and return to biblical ways. But it can be done. Every now and then in the past Christians have had to do it. History has recorded several large-scale returns led by such men as St. Francis, Martin Luther, and George Fox. Unfortunately, there seems to be no Luther or Fox on the horizon at present. Whether or not another such return may be expected before the coming of Christ is a question upon which Christians are not fully agreed, but that is not of too great importance to us now.

What God in His sovereignty may yet do on a world-scale I do not claim to know. But what He will do for the plain man or woman who seeks His face I believe I do know and can tell others. Let any man turn to God in earnest, let him begin to exercise himself unto godliness, let him seek to develop his powers of spiritual receptivity by trust and obedience and humility, and the results will exceed anything he may have hoped in his leaner and weaker days.

Any man who by repentance and a sincere return to God will break himself out of the mold in which he has been held, and will go to the Bible itself for his spiritual standards, will be delighted with what he finds there.

DAY 19

WE MUST DIE IF
WE WOULD LIVE

*I have been crucified with Christ
and I no longer live, but Christ lives in me.*

GALATIANS 2:20

Let me die—lest I die—only let me see Thy face." That was the prayer of St. Augustine.

"Hide not Thy face from me," he cried in an agony of desire. "Oh! That I might repose on Thee. Oh! That Thou wouldst enter into my heart, and inebriate it, that I may not forget my ills, and embrace Thee, my sole good."

This longing to die, to get our opaque form out of the way so that it might not hide from us the lovely face of God, is one that is instantly understood by the hungry-hearted believer. To die that we might not die! There is no contradiction here, for there are before us two kinds of dying, a dying to be sought and a dying to be avoided at any cost.

To Augustine the sight of God inwardly enjoyed was life itself and anything less than that was death. To exist in total eclipse under the shadow of nature without the realized Presence was a condition not to be tolerated. Whatever hid God's face from him must be taken out of the way, even his own self-love, his dearest ego, his most cherished treasures. So he prayed, "Let me die."

The great saint's daring prayer was heard and, as might be expected, was answered with a fullness of generosity characteristic of God. He died the kind of death to which Paul testified: "I am crucified with Christ: nevertheless I live; yet not I, but Christ liveth in me" (Galatians 2:20). His life and ministry continued and his presence is always there, in his books, in the church, in history; but wondrous as it may be, he is strangely transparent; his own personality is scarcely seen, while the light of Christ shines through with a kind of healing splendor.

There have been those who have thought that to get themselves out of the way it was necessary to withdraw from society; so they denied all natural human relationships and went into the desert or the mountain or the hermit's cell to fast and labor and struggle to mortify their flesh. While their motive was good it is impossible to commend their method. It is altogether too tough to be killed by abusing the body or starving the affections. It yields to nothing less than the cross.

In every Christian's heart there is a cross and a throne, and the Christian is on the throne till he puts himself on the cross; if he refuses the cross he remains on the throne. Perhaps this is at the bottom of the backsliding and worldliness among gospel believers today. We want to be saved but we insist that Christ do all the dying. No cross for us, no dethronement, no dying. We remain king within the little kingdom of Mansoul and wear our tinsel crown with all the pride of a Caesar; but we doom ourselves to shadows and weakness and spiritual sterility.

If we will not die then we must die, and that death will mean the forfeiture of many of those everlasting treasures which the saints have cherished. Our uncrucified flesh will rob us of purity of heart, Christlikeness of character, spiritual insight, fruitfulness; and more than all, it will hide from us the vision of God's face, that vision which has been the light of earth and will be the completeness of heaven.

THE GAZE
OF THE SOUL

One thing I ask from the Lord, this only do I seek: that I may dwell in the house of the Lord all the days of my life, to gaze on the beauty of the Lord and to seek him in his temple.

PSALM 27:4

Those who look to him are radiant;
their faces are never covered with shame.

PSALM 34:5

When we lift our inward eyes to gaze upon God we are sure to meet friendly eyes gazing back at us, for it is written that the eyes of the Lord run to and fro throughout all the earth. The sweet language of experience is "Thou God seest me" (Genesis 16:13). When the eyes of the soul looking out meet the eyes of God looking in, heaven has begun right here on this earth. Nicholas of Cusa wrote five hundred years ago:

> When all my endeavor is turned toward Thee
> because all Thy endeavor is turned toward
> me; when I look unto Thee alone with all my
> attention, nor ever turn aside the eyes of my
> mind, because Thou dost enfold me with Thy
> constant regard; when I direct my love toward
> Thee alone because Thou, who art Love's self
> hast turned Thee toward me alone. And what,
> Lord, is my life, save that embrace wherein
> Thy delightsome sweetness doth so lovingly
> enfold me?

I should like to say more about this old man of God. He is not much known today anywhere among Christian believers, and among current fundamentalists he is known not at all. I feel that we could gain much from a little acquaintance with men of his spiritual flavor and the school of Christian thought which they represent. Christian literature, to be accepted and approved by evangelical leaders of our times, must follow very closely the same train of thought, a kind of "party line" from which it is scarcely safe to depart. A half-century of this in America has made us smug and content. We imitate each other with slavish devotion. Our most strenuous efforts are put forth to try to say the same thing that everyone around us is saying—and yet to find an excuse for saying it, some little safe variation on the approved theme or, if no more, at least a new illustration.

Nicholas was a true follower of Christ, a lover of the Lord, radiant and shining in his devotion to the person of Jesus. His theology was orthodox but fragrant and sweet as everything about Jesus might properly be expected to be. His conception of eternal life, for instance, is beautiful in itself and, if I mistake not, is nearer in spirit to John 17:3 than that which is current among us today. Life eternal, says Nicholas, is

> nought other than that blessed regard wherewith Thou never ceasest to behold me, yes, even the secret places of my soul. With Thee, to behold is to give life; 'tis unceasingly to impart sweetest love of Thee 'tis to inflame me to love of Thee by love's imparting, and to feed me by inflaming, and by feeding to kindle my yearning, and by kindling to make me drink of the dew of gladness, and by drinking to infuse in me a fountain of life, and by infusing to make it increase and endure.

Now, if faith is the gaze of the heart at God, and if this gaze is but the raising of the inward eyes to meet the all-seeing eyes of God, then it follows that it is one of the easiest things possible to do. It would be like God to make the most vital thing easy and place it within the range of possibility for the weakest and poorest of us.

MORTIFY THE FLESH

*Put to death, therefore, whatever belongs to your
earthly nature: sexual immorality, impurity, lust,
evil desires and greed, which is idolatry.*

COLOSSIANS 3:5

I n these terrible days in which we live, we have not only
accepted the flesh in its morally fine manifestation as
being quite proper, but we have created an ignoble theology of "extenuating circumstances" by which we excuse
the flesh.

People do not hesitate any more to say, "Oh, was I
mad!" and then a minute later, lead in prayer. But he is
just mumbling words. I have no confidence in a man
who loses his temper. I do not believe that a man who
blows up and loses his temper is a spiritual man, whether
he is a preacher, a bishop, or a pope. He is a carnal man

and needs to be cleansed by fire and blood. But we have excused people who say, "I was mad." If you were mad, you were sinning and you need to be cleansed from your bad temper. But we have incorporated the flesh into our orthodoxy, and instead of being humble, we magnify the proud fellow.

Years ago God gave me an ice pick and said, "Now son, among your other duties will be to puncture all the inflated egos you see. Go stick an ice pick in them." And there has been more popping and hissing in my ministry as the air goes out of egos. People hate me for that, but I love them for the privilege of whittling them down to size, because if there is anything that we ought to get straight, it is how little we are.

When I was a young fellow, I always loved guns. I had a .22 revolver and loved to shoot. Just for fun when I had nothing else to do, and that is rare now, I would go out shooting with another fellow, and we shot what we called a mud hen. It looked like a great big duck, but when we dressed it, it was the biggest hypocrite you ever saw. It was practically all feathers. It was not much bigger than an oversized robin when we got down to the real bird. That describes most Christians. We stand our feathers on end so people do not know how small we are.

The word *mortify* comes from the same Latin word as *mortuary*—a place where you put dead people. It means "to die." But we do not talk about that much any more. We talk about it, but we do not believe in getting reduced.

But you will never be a spiritual man until God reduces you to your proper size.

Mortify is a New Testament word. Turn your back upon yourself and reckon yourself to be dead indeed and crucified with Christ. Then expect the blood of Christ and the power of the Holy Spirit to make real what your faith has reckoned. And then begin to live it. Some people go to an altar and get sanctified, but they're still resentful, they still have a chip on their shoulder. They still love money. They still have a temper. They still look where they should not. And then they claim to be sanctified. They are just pretenders, or worse than that, they are deceived persons. Either we mortify the flesh or the flesh will harm us to a point where we have no power, no joy, no fruit, no usefulness, no victory.

DAY 22

THE SANCTIFICATION
OF OUR DESIRES

*Blessed are those who hunger and thirst
for righteousness, for they will be filled.*

MATTHEW 5:6

I n nature it is easy to watch the activity carried on by
desire. The very perpetuation of the various species is
guaranteed by the presence of desire, and each individual
member of each species is sustained and nourished by the
natural operation of desire. Every normal creature desires
to mate, and so the perpetuation of life is achieved. Every
creature desires food, and the life of each is supported.
Thus desire is the servant of the God of nature and waits
on His will.

In the moral world things are not otherwise. Right

desires tend toward life and evil ones toward death.
That in essence is the scriptural teaching on this subject.
Whatever a man wants badly and persistently enough will
determine the man's character. In the Pauline epistles the
gravitational pull of the heart in one direction or another
is called the "mind." In the eighth chapter of Romans, for
instance, when Paul refers to the "mind" he is referring
to the sum of our dominant desires. The mere intellect is
not the mind: the mind is intellect plus an emotional tug
strong enough to determine action.

By this definition it is easy to understand the words of
Romans 8:5–7:

> For they that are after the flesh do mind the
> things of the flesh; but they that are after the
> Spirit the things of the Spirit. For to be car-
> nally minded is death; but to be spiritually
> minded is life and peace. Because the carnal
> mind is enmity against God: for it is not sub-
> ject to the law of God, neither indeed can be.

When our dominant desires are bad the whole life is
bad as a consequence; when the desires are good the life
comes up to the level of our desires, provided that we
have within us the enabling Spirit.

At the root of all true spiritual growth is a set of right
and sanctified desires. The whole Bible teaches that we
can have whatever we want badly enough if, it hardly need

be said, our desire is according to the will of God. The desire after God and holiness is back of all real spirituality, and when that desire becomes dominant in the life nothing can prevent us from having what we want. The longing cry of the God-hungry soul can be expressed in the five words of the song, "Oh, to Be Like Thee!" While this longing persists there will be steady growth in grace and a constant progress toward Christlikeness.

Unsanctified desire will stop the growth of any Christian life. Wrong desire perverts the moral judgment so that we are unable to appraise the desired object at its real value. However we try, still a thing looks morally better because we want it. For that reason our heart is often our worst counselor, for if it is filled with desire it may give us bad advice, pleading the purity of something that is in itself anything but pure.

As Christians our only safety lies in complete honesty. We must surrender our hearts to God so that we have no unholy desires, then let the Scriptures pronounce their judgment on a contemplated course. If the Scriptures condemn an object, we must accept that judgment and conform to it, no matter how we may for the moment feel about it.

Week 5

NO SAVIORHOOD
WITHOUT LORDSHIP

For I am the Lord your God,
the Holy One of Israel, your Savior...

ISAIAH 43:3

... our Lord and Savior Jesus Christ ...

2 PETER 2:20

Mankind appears to have a positive genius for twisting truth until it ceases to be truth and becomes downright falsehood. By overemphasizing in one place and underemphasizing in another the whole pattern of truth may be so altered that a completely false view results without our being aware of it.

This fact was brought forcibly to mind recently by

hearing again the discredited doctrine of a divided Christ so widely accepted in many religious circles. It goes like this: Christ is both Savior and Lord. A sinner may be saved by accepting Him as Savior without yielding to Him as Lord. The practical outworking of this doctrine is that the evangelist presents and the seeker accepts a divided Christ. We have all heard the tearful plea made to persons already saved to accept Christ as Lord and thus enter into the victorious life.

Almost all deeper life teaching is based upon this fallacy, but because it contains a germ of truth its soundness is not questioned. Anyway, it is extremely simple and quite popular, and in addition to these selling points it is also ready-made for both speaker and hearer and requires no thinking by either. So sermons embodying this heresy are freely preached, books are written, and songs composed, all saying the same thing; and all saying the wrong thing, except, as I have said, for a feeble germ of truth lying inert at the bottom.

Now, it seems odd that none of these teachers ever noticed that the only true object of saving faith is none other than Christ Himself; not the "saviorhood" of Christ nor the "lordship" of Christ, but Christ Himself. God does not offer salvation to the one who will believe on one of the offices of Christ, nor is an office of Christ ever presented as an object of faith. Neither are we exhorted to believe on the atonement, nor on the cross, nor on the priesthood of the Savior. All of these are embodied in the person of Christ, but they are never separated nor is one ever isolated from the rest. Much less are we permitted to accept one of Christ's offices and reject another. The notion that we are so permitted is a modern-day heresy, I repeat, and like every heresy it has had evil consequences among Christians. No heresy is ever entertained with impunity. We pay in practical failure for our theoretical errors.

It is altogether doubtful whether any man can be saved who comes to Christ for His help but with no intention to obey Him. Christ's saviorhood is forever united to His lordship. Look at the Scriptures:

> If thou shalt confess with thy mouth the
> Lord Jesus, and shalt believe in thine heart that
> God hath raised him from the dead, thou shalt
> be saved. . . . For the same Lord over all is rich
> unto all that call upon him. For whosoever shall
> call upon the name of the Lord shall be saved.
> ROMANS 10:9, 12–13

There the *Lord* is the object of faith for salvation. And when the Philippian jailer asked the way to be saved, Paul replied, "Believe on the Lord Jesus Christ, and thou shalt be saved" (Acts 16:31). He did not tell him to believe on the Savior with the thought that he could later take up the matter of His lordship and settle it at his own convenience. To Paul there could be no division of offices.

Christ must be Lord or He will not be Savior.

There is no intention here to teach that the earnest believer may not go on to explore ever-increasing meanings in Christ, nor do we hold that our first saving contact with Christ brings perfect knowledge of all He is to us. The contrary is true. Ages upon ages will hardly be long enough to allow us to experience all the riches of His grace. As we discover new meanings in His titles and make them ours, we will grow in the knowledge of our Lord and in personal appreciation of the multifold offices He fills and the many forms of love He wears exalted on His throne. That is the truth which has been twisted out of shape and reduced to impotence by the doctrine that we can believe on His saviorhood while rejecting His lordship.

CRUCIFIED
WITH CHRIST

*I have been crucified with Christ and I no
longer live, but Christ lives in me. The life I now
live in the body, I live by faith in the Son of God,
who loved me and gave himself for me.*

GALATIANS 2:20

I t is plain in this text that Paul was forthright and frank
in the matter of his own personal involvement in
seeking and finding God's highest desires and provision
for Christian experience and victory. He was not bashful
about the implications of his own personality becoming
involved with the claims of Jesus Christ.

Not only does he plainly testify, "I have been crucified,"
but within the immediate vicinity of these verses, he used

the words *I*, *myself*, and *me* a total of fourteen times.

I believe Paul knew that there is a legitimate time and place for the use of the word *I*. In spiritual matters, some people seem to want to maintain a kind of anonymity, if possible. As far as they are concerned, someone else should take the first step. This often comes up in the manner of our praying, as well. Some Christians are so general and vague and uninvolved in their requests that God Himself is unable to answer. I refer to the man who will bow his head and pray: "Lord, bless the missionaries and all for whom we should pray. Amen."

It is as though Paul says to us here: "I am not ashamed to use myself as an example. I have been crucified with Christ. I am willing to be pinpointed."

Only Christianity recognizes why the person who is without God and without any spiritual perception gets in such deep trouble with his own ego. When he says *I*, he is talking about the sum of his own individual being, and if he does not really know who he is or what he is doing here, he is besieged in his personality with all kinds of questions and problems and uncertainties.

Most of the shallow psychology religions of the day try to deal with the problem of the ego by jockeying it around from one position to another, but Christianity deals with the problem of *I* by disposing of it with finality.

The Bible teaches that every unregenerated human being will continue to wrestle with the problems of his own natural ego and selfishness. His human nature dates back to Adam. But the Bible also teaches with joy and blessing that every individual may be born again, thus becoming a "new man" in Christ.

When Paul speaks in this text, "I have been crucified," he is saying that "my natural self has been crucified." That is why he can go on to say, "Yet I live"—for he has become another and a new person—"I live in Christ and Christ lives in me."

PRAISE GOD
FOR THE FURNACE

Consider it pure joy, my brothers and sisters,
whenever you face trials of many kinds, because you know
that the testing of your faith produces perseverance.

JAMES 1:2–3

It was the enraptured Rutherford who could shout in the midst of serious and painful trials, "Praise God for the hammer, the file, and the furnace."

The hammer is a useful tool, but the nail, if it had feeling and intelligence could present another side of the story. For the nail knows the hammer only as an opponent, a brutal, merciless enemy who lives to pound it into submission, to beat it down out of sight, and clinch it into place. That is the nail's view of the hammer, and it is accurate except for one thing: the nail forgets that both it and the hammer are servants of the same workman. Let the nail but remember that the hammer is held by the workman and all resentment toward it will disappear. The carpenter decides whose head shall be beaten next and what hammer shall be used in the beating. That is his sovereign right. When the nail has surrendered to the will of the workman and has gotten a little glimpse of his benign plans for its future, it will yield to the hammer without complaint.

The file is more painful still, for its business is to bite into the soft metal, scraping and eating away the edges till it has shaped the metal to its will. Yet the file has, in truth, no real will in the matter, but serves another master as the metal also does. It is the master and not the file that decides how much shall be eaten away, what shape the metal shall take, and how long the painful filing shall continue. Let the metal accept the will of the master and it will not try to dictate when or how it shall be filed.

As for the furnace, it is the worst of all. Ruthless and savage, it leaps at every combustible thing that enters it and never relaxes its fury till it has reduced it all to shapeless ashes. All that refuses to burn is melted to a mass of helpless matter, without will or purpose of its own. When everything is melted that will melt and all is burned that will burn, then and not till then the furnace calms down and rests from its destructive fury.

With all this known to him, how could Rutherford

find it in his heart to praise God for the hammer, the file, and the furnace? The answer is simply that he loved the Master of the hammer, he adored the Workman who wielded the file, he worshiped the Lord who heated the furnace for the everlasting blessing of His children. He had felt the hammer till its rough beatings no longer hurt; he had endured the file till he had come actually to enjoy its bitings; he had walked with God in the furnace so long that it had become as his natural habitat. That does not overstate the facts. His letters reveal as much.

Such doctrine as this does not find much sympathy among Christians in these soft and carnal days. We tend to think of Christianity as a painless system by which we can escape the penalty of past sins and attain to heaven at last. The flaming desire to be rid of every unholy thing and to put on the likeness of Christ at any cost is not often found among us. We expect to enter the everlasting kingdom of our Father and to sit down around the table with sages, saints, and martyrs; and through the grace of God, maybe we shall; yes, maybe we shall.

But for most of us it could prove at first an embarrassing experience. Ours might be the silence of the untried soldier in the presence of the battle-hardened heroes who have fought the fight and won the victory and who have scars to prove that they were present when the battle was joined.

DAY 26

THE FRUITS
OF OBEDIENCE

*. . . so that all the Gentiles might come
to the obedience that comes from faith . . .*

ROMANS 16:26

The Church of our day has soft-pedaled the doctrine of obedience, either neglecting it altogether or mentioning it only apologetically and without urgency. This results from a fundamental confusion of obedience with works in the minds of preacher and people. To escape the error of salvation by works we have fallen into the opposite error of salvation without obedience. In our eagerness to get rid of the legalistic doctrine of works we have thrown out the baby with the bathwater and gotten rid of obedience as well.

The Bible knows nothing of salvation apart from obedience. Paul testified that he was sent to preach "obedience to the faith among all nations" (Romans 1:5). He reminded the Roman Christians that they had been set free from sin because they had "obeyed from the heart that form of doctrine which was delivered you" (Romans 6:17). In the New Testament there is no contradiction between faith and obedience. Between faith and law-works, yes; between law and grace, yes; but between faith and obedience, not at all. The Bible recognizes no faith that does not lead to obedience, nor does it recognize any obedience that does not spring from faith. The two are opposite sides of the same coin. Were we to split a coin edgewise we would destroy both sides and render the whole thing valueless. So faith and obedience are forever joined and each one is without value when separated from the other. The trouble with many of us today is that we are trying to believe without intending to obey.

The message of the cross contains two elements: (1) promises and declarations to be believed, and (2) commandments to be obeyed. Obviously faith is necessary to the first and obedience to the second. The only thing we can do with a promise or statement of fact is to believe it; it is physically impossible to obey it, for it is not addressed to the will, but to the understanding. It is equally impossible to believe a command; it is not addressed to our understanding, but to our will. True, we may have faith in its justice; we may have confidence that it is a good and right command, but that is not enough. Until we have either obeyed or refused to obey we have not done anything about it yet. To strain to exercise faith toward that which is addressed to our obedience is to get ourselves tangled in a maze of impossibilities.

The doctrine of Christ crucified and the wealth of truths which cluster around it have in them this dual content. So the apostle could speak of "obedience to the faith" without talking contradictions. And it can be said, "The gospel is the power of God unto salvation to everyone that *believeth*," and "He became the author of eternal salvation unto all them that obey Him." There is nothing incompatible between these statements when they are understood in the light of the essential unity of faith and obedience.

THE NEED FOR SELF-JUDGMENT

We are those who have died to sin;
how can we live in it any longer?

ROMANS 6:2

Between deeds and consequences there is a relationship as close and inescapable as that which exists between the seed and the harvest.

We are moral beings and as such we must accept the consequence of every deed done and every word spoken. We cannot act apart from the concept of right and wrong. By our very nature we are compelled to own a three-dimensional moral obligation every time we exercise the right of choice; namely, the obligation to God, to ourselves, and to others. No conscious moral being can be imagined to exist for even one moment in a nonmoral situation.

The whole question of right and wrong, of moral responsibility, of justice and judgment, and of reward and punishment, is sharply accented for us by the fact that we are members of a fallen race, occupying a position halfway between hell and heaven, with the knowledge of good and evil inherent within our intricate natures, along with ability to turn toward good and an inborn propensity to turn toward evil.

The present state of the human race before God is probationary. The world is on trial. The voice of God sounds over the earth, "Behold I set before you the way of life and the way of death. Choose you this day" (Jeremiah 21:8).

It has been held by most Jews and Christians that the period of probation for the individual ends with his death and after that comes the judgment. This belief is supported completely by the Scriptures of the Old and New Testaments, and any variance from this view is the result of the introduction of non-scriptural concepts into Christian thinking.

The cross of Christ has altered somewhat the position of certain persons before the judgment of God. Toward those who embrace the provisions of mercy that center around the death and resurrection of Christ one phase of judgment is no longer operative. "He that heareth my word, and believeth on him that sent me, hath everlasting life, and shall not come into condemnation; but is passed from death unto life" (John 5:24).

That is the way our Lord stated this truth, and we have only to know that the word *condemned* as it occurs here is actually "judgment" to see that for believers the consequences of sinful deeds have, in at least one aspect, been remitted.

When Christ died in the darkness for us men He made it possible for God to remit the penalty of the broken law, reestablish repentant sinners in His favor exactly as if they had never sinned and do the whole thing without relaxing the severity of the law or compromising the high demands of justice (see Romans 3:24–26).

This is a mystery too high for us, and we honor God more by believing without understanding than by trying to understand. The Just died for the unjust; and because He did, the unjust may now live with the Just in complete moral congruity. Thanks be to God for His unspeakable gift.

Does this mean that the redeemed man has no responsibility to God for his conduct? Does it mean that now that he is clothed with the righteousness of Christ he will never be called to account for his deeds? God forbid! How could the moral Governor of the universe release a segment of that universe from the moral law of deeds and consequences and hope to uphold the order of the world?

Within the household of God among the redeemed and justified there is law as well as grace; not the law of Moses that knew no mercy, but the kindly law of the Father's heart that requires and expects of His children lives lived in conformity to the commandments of Christ.

THE CROSS IS
A RADICAL THING

*Whoever wants to be my disciple must deny
themselves and take up their cross and follow me.*

MATTHEW 16:24

The cross of Christ is the most revolutionary thing
ever to appear among men.

The cross of old Roman times knew no compromise; it
never made concessions. It won all its arguments by kill-
ing its opponent and silencing him for good. It spared not
Christ, but slew Him the same as the rest. He was alive
when they hung Him on that cross and completely dead
when they took Him down six hours later. That was the
cross the first time it appeared in Christian history.

After Christ was risen from the dead the apostles

went out to preach His message, and what they preached was the cross. And wherever they went into the wide world they carried the cross, and the same revolutionary power went with them. The radical message of the cross transformed Saul of Tarsus and changed him from a persecutor of Christians to a tender believer and an apostle of the faith. Its power changed bad men into good ones. It shook off the long bondage of paganism and altered completely the whole moral and mental outlook of the Western world.

All this it did and continued to do as long as it was permitted to remain what it had been originally—a cross. Its power departed when it was changed from a thing of death to a thing of beauty. When men made of it a symbol, hung it around their necks as an ornament or made its outline before their faces as a magic sign to ward off evil, then it became at best a weak emblem, at worst a positive fetish. As such it is revered today by millions who know absolutely nothing about its power.

The cross effects its ends by destroying one established pattern, the victim's, and creating another pattern, its own. Thus it always has its way. It wins by defeating its opponent and imposing its will upon him. It always dominates. It never compromises, never dickers nor confers, never surrenders a point for the sake of peace. It cares not for peace; it cares only to end its opposition as fast as possible.

With perfect knowledge of all this Christ said, "If any man will come after me, let him deny himself, and take up his cross, and follow me" (Matthew 16:24). So the cross not only brings Christ's life to an end, it ends also the first life, the old life, of every one of His true followers. It destroys the old pattern, the Adam pattern, in the believer's life, and brings it to an end. Then the God who raised Christ from the dead raises the believer and a new life begins.

Week 6

DAY 29

FOLLOWING
THE LORD

*I am the light of the world. Whoever follows me will
never walk in darkness, but will have the light of life.*

JOHN 8:12

*We know that we have come to
know him if we keep his commands.*

I JOHN 2:3

We are always in danger of falling victim to words.
An unctuous phrase may easily take the place of
spiritual reality. One example is the expression "Following
the Lord" so often used among Christians, or its variation, "Following the Lamb." We overlook the fact that this
cannot be taken literally. We cannot now, as those first

disciples could, follow the Master over a given geographical area. We tend to think of it literally but at the same time *feel* its literal impossibility, with the result that it has come to mean little more than a nodded agreement to the truths of Christianity. It may startle us to learn that *following* is a New Testament word used to cover the idea of an established habit of obedience to the commandments of Christ.

Look at the fruits of obedience as described in the New Testament: The house of the obedient man is built upon a rock (Matthew 7:24). He shall be loved by the Father and shall have the manifestation of the Father and the Son, who will come unto him and make their abode with him (John 14:21, 23). He shall abide in the love of Christ (John 15:10). By obedience to the doctrines of Christ he is set free from sin and made a servant of righteousness (Romans 6:17–18). The Holy Spirit is given to him (Acts 5:32). He is delivered from self-deception and blessed in his deeds (James 1:22–25). His faith is perfected (James 2:22). He is confirmed in his assurance toward God and given confidence in prayer, so that what he asks is given to him (1 John 3:18–22). These are only a few among the many verses that may be cited from the New Testament. But more to the point than any number of proof texts is the fact that the whole drift of the New Testament is in that direction. One or two texts might be misunderstood, but there is no mistaking the whole tenor of Scripture.

What does all this add up to? What are its practical

implications for us today? Just that the power of God is at our disposal, waiting for us to call it into action by meeting the conditions which are plainly laid down. God is ready to send down floods of blessing upon us as we begin to obey His plain instructions. We need no new doctrine, no new movement, no "key," no imported evangelist or expensive "course" to show us the way. It is before us as clear as a four-lane highway.

To any inquirer I would say, "Just do the next thing you know you should do to carry out the will of the Lord. If there is sin in your life, quit it instantly. Put away lying, gossiping, dishonesty, or whatever your sin may be. Forsake worldly pleasures, extravagance in spending, vanity in dress, in your car, in your home. Get right with any person you may have wronged. Forgive everyone who may have wronged you. Begin to use your money to help the poor and advance the cause of Christ. Take up the cross and live sacrificially. Pray, attend the Lord's services. Witness for Christ, not only when it is convenient but when you know you should. Look to no cost and fear no consequences. Study the Bible to learn the will of God and then do His will as you understand it. Start now by doing the next thing, and then go on from there."

THE CROSS
DOES INTERFERE

Whoever wants to be my disciple must deny themselves and take up their cross daily and follow me.

LUKE 9:23

Things have come to a pretty pass," said a famous Englishman testily, "when religion is permitted to interfere with our private lives."

To which we may reply that things have come to a worse pass when an intelligent man living in a Protestant country could make such a remark. Had this man never read the New Testament? Had he never heard of Stephen or Paul or Peter? Had he never thought about the millions who followed Christ cheerfully to violent deaths, sudden

or lingering, because they *did* allow their religion to interfere with their private lives?

But we must leave this man to his conscience and
his Judge and look into our own hearts. Maybe he but
expressed openly what some of us feel secretly. Just how
radically has our religion interfered with the neat pattern
of our own lives? Perhaps we had better answer that question first.

I have long believed that a man who spurns the
Christian faith outright is more respected before God
and the heavenly powers than the man who pretends to
be religious but refuses to come under its total domina-
tion. The first is an overt enemy, the second a false friend.
It is the latter who will be spewed out of the mouth of
Christ; and the reason is not hard to understand.

One picture of a Christian is a man carrying a cross.
"If any man will come after me, let him deny himself, and
take up his cross daily, and follow me" (Luke 9:23). The
man with a cross no longer controls his destiny; he lost
control when he picked up his cross. That cross immediately became to him an all-absorbing interest, an over-
whelming interference. No matter what he may desire
to do, there is but one thing he *can* do; that is, move on
toward the place of crucifixion.

The man who will not tolerate interference is under no
compulsion to follow Christ. "If any man will," said our
Lord, and thus freed every man and placed the Christian
life in the realm of voluntary choice.

Yet no man can escape interference. Law, duty, hunger, accident, natural disasters, illness, death, all intrude into his plans, and in the long run there is nothing he can do about it. Long experience with the rude necessities of life has taught men that these interferences will be thrust upon them sooner or later, so they learn to make what terms they can with the inevitable. They learn how to stay within the narrow circular rabbit path where the least interference is to be found. The bolder ones may challenge the world, enlarge the circle somewhat and so increase the number of their problems, but no one invites trouble deliberately. Human nature is not built that way. . . .

But we must not get the impression that the Christian life is one continuous conflict, one unbroken irritating struggle against the world, the flesh, and the devil. A thousand times no. The heart that learns to die with Christ soon knows the blessed experience of rising with Him, and all the world's persecutions cannot still the high note of holy joy that springs up in the soul that has become the dwelling place of the Holy Spirit.

GOD STANDS READY

Submit yourselves, then, to God.
Resist the devil, and he will flee from you.

JAMES 4:7

God is saying, "I stand ready to pour a little liquid fire into your heart, into your spiritual being!"

We respond: "No, Lord, please excuse me. That sounds like fanaticism—and I would have to give up some things!" So we refuse His desire, even though we want all the benefits of His cross.

There is this thoughtful phrase in *The Cloud of Unknowing**: "He wills thou do but look on Him and let Him alone." Let God alone. In other words, let Him work! Don't stop Him. Don't prevent Him from kindling your heart, from blessing you and leading you out of a common state into that of special longing after Him. You don't have to coax God. He is not like a reluctant father waiting for his child to beg. The blessings are His to give and He waits for us to let Him work.

This is a very hard thing for Americans to do because we are naturally born "do-it-yourself" artists! We don't just hire a plumber and let him do his work—we stand by and tell him how it should be done. It is amazing really that any American ever lies down and allows the doctor to perform the operation. We always want to get our finger in, and that is the way most Christians behave. We think God does the really hard jobs, but that He is glad to have us along to help out.

"Look on Him—and let Him work, let Him alone." Get your hands down to your side and stop trying to tell God where to cut. Stop trying to make the diagnosis for God. Stop trying to tell God what to give you. He is the Physician! You are the patient.

This is good doctrine, brethren. Dr. A. B. Simpson shocked and blessed and helped dear people in all Christian groups as he taught his truth down through the years—"Let God work! Let Him alone! Take your hands off! It is God that worketh in you!"

Let Him work and your spiritual life will begin to blaze like the rising sun.

Note:

* An anonymous work on contemplative prayer written in Middle English in the latter half of the fourteenth century.

"IT WILL COST YOU NOTHING"

The kingdom of heaven is like treasure hidden in a field.
When a man found it, he hid it again, and then in his joy
went and sold all he had and bought that field.

MATTHEW 13:44

I n our day, there is a tendency for enthusiastic
Christian promoters to teach that the essence of faith
is this: "Come to Jesus—it will cost you nothing! The
price has all been paid—it will cost you nothing!"

Brethren, that is a dangerous half-truth. There
is always a price connected with salvation and with
discipleship.

But some will say: "Isn't that what the missionaries

teach all around the world? Don't they say, 'Come! Everything is free. Jesus paid it all'?"

God's grace is free, no doubt about that. No one in the wide world can make any human payment towards the plea of salvation or the forgiveness of sins.

But I know the missionaries well enough to know that they would never go to people anywhere in the world and simply teach: "You do not have to do a thing. Your faith in Jesus Christ will never cost you anything."

I have been receiving a magazine in the mail—someone sends it to me in a plain wrapper with no return address. I wish he or she would stop sending it.

The man who edits this paper also preaches on the radio, and the philosophy he spreads is this: "Everybody in the world has faith. All you have to do is turn your faith loose in the right direction. Turn it towards Christ and everything is all fixed up!"

Now, that is truly a misconception of what the Bible says about man and about God and about faith. It is a misconception fostered by the devil himself.

The Apostle Paul told believers plainly and clearly that "not everyone has faith."

Actually, faith is a rare plant. Faith is not a plant that grows everywhere by the way. It is not a common plant that belongs to everyone. Faith is a rare and wonderful plant that lives and grows only in the penitent soul.

The teaching that everyone has faith and all you have to do is use it is simply a form of humanism in the guise of Christianity. I warn you that any faith that belongs to everybody is a humanistic faith and it is not the faith that saves. It is not that faith which is a gift of God to a broken heart.

I think it must be apparent to us that Nicodemus, a ruler in Israel, would have known what it might cost him to inquire of Jesus about the things of faith and of God's plan and of eternal life. He was feeling his way.

RAISED WITH CHRIST

Since, then, you have been raised with Christ . . .

COLOSSIANS 3:1

God takes pleasure in confounding everything that comes under the guise of human power—which is really weakness disguised! Our intellectual power, our great mind, our array of talents—all of these are good if God has so ordered, but in reality they are human weaknesses disguised. God wants to crucify us from head to foot—making our own powers ridiculous and useless—in the desire to raise us without measure for His glory and for our eternal good.

Dare we realize what a gracious thing it is that the Lord of all creation is desirous of raising us into a position of such glory and usefulness? Can we conceive that God would speak to angels and all the creatures who do His will and say of us: "The lid is off for this child of mine! There is to be no ceiling, no measure on what he can have, and there is no limit to where I may take him. Just keep it open. Without measure I will raise him because without pity I have been able to crucify him!"

You who are parents and you who have had the care of children know what it is to chasten without pity and yet at the same time discipline and punish with both love and pity. What do you do when you want your child to be the very finest example of manhood and character and citizenship? You pray for him and you love him so much that you would give the blood out of your veins for him—yet without pity you apply the rod of discipline and chastening. It is actually pity that makes you punish him without pity!

That sounds like a beautiful mix-up, but that is the character and desire of our God for us if we are His children. It is the love and the pity of God for His children that prescribes the chastening of a cross so that we may become the kind of mature believers and disciples that He wants us to be.

I earnestly believe that God is trying to raise up a company of Christians in our day who are willing to be completely separated from all prejudices and all carnal desires. He wants those who are ready to put themselves at God's disposal, willing to bear any kind of cross—iron or lead or straw or gold or whatever—and to be the kinds of examples He needs on this earth.

The great question is: Is there a readiness, an eagerness among us for the kind of cross He wants to reveal through us?

Often we sing, "Hold Thou Thy cross before my closing eyes; / Shine through the gloom and point me to the skies."

What a pathetic thing to see the cross so misunderstood in sections of Christianity. Think of poor souls who have never found the evangelical meaning and assurance of atonement and justification, cleansing, and pardon. When they come to the time of death, the best they know is to clutch some manufactured cross to the breast, holding it tightly and hoping for some power to come from painted metal or carved wood to take them safely over the river.

No, no! That is not the kind of cross that helps. The cross that we want is that which will come to us from being in the will of God. It is not a cross on a hill nor a cross on a church. It is not the cross that can be worn around the neck. It must be the cross of obedience to the will of God, and we must embrace it, each believer for himself!

CHRIST IS THE PATTERN

And we all, who with unveiled faces contemplate the Lord's glory, are being transformed into his image with ever-increasing glory, which comes from the Lord, who is the Spirit.

2 CORINTHIANS 3:18

The message of Christ lays hold upon a man with the intention to alter him, to mold him again and again after another image, and make of him something altogether different from what he had been before. "Be ye transformed by the renewing of your mind" (Romans 12:2) is the injunction laid upon believing men by the apostle.

Now, granted that men may be changed and that the power of God in the gospel can change them, the important questions naturally are, Into what image are they to be changed? Who or what is to be the model for them?

To these questions there have been many answers given. The quasi-Christian religious philosophy so popular today answers that there is a "norm" somewhere in human nature from which we have departed to a greater or lesser degree and to which we must be restored. So religion is brought in to aid in the restoration. It operates by "adjusting" the inquiring soul, first to himself and then to society. Everything depends upon this work of adjustment. Human nature, so runs the theory, is basically right and good, but it has been put out of focus by the world stresses in which it is compelled to live. It has been warped by environment, by bad teaching, and by various harmful influences, beginning at the time of its birth or before.

The whole burden of this type of religious thinking is to restore the man to an image of himself. All he needs is to be made into his own likeness again, to become a "real person," free from the warping influences of prejudice, fear, and superstition. He was all right to begin with, as were his ancestors before him, and his highest present goal is to be restored, like a damaged painting, so that the hand of the Master may again be discovered under the soil and grime of life.

All this sounds just cozy, but the trouble is that the underlying idea is completely false, and all the religious hopes and dreams arising from it are and must be without foundation.

The message of the New Testament is bluntly opposite to this. People are *not* all right except for minor maladjustments. They are lost, inwardly lost, morally and spiritually lost. That has been the persistent Christian testimony from the first, and human history has shown how correct it is. There is nothing in us that can serve as a model for the new man. Conformity to ourselves, even our better selves, can lead only to ultimate tragedy. "The [human] heart is deceitful above all things, and desperately wicked" (Jeremiah 17:9). It must have help from outside itself, from above itself, if it is to escape the gravitational pull of its own sinful nature. And this help the gospel furnishes in full and sufficient measure.

The gospel not only furnishes transforming power to remold the human heart; it provides also a model after which the new life is to be fashioned, and that model is Christ Himself. Christ is God acting like God in the lowly raiments of human flesh. Yet He is also man; so He becomes the perfect model after which redeemed human nature is to be fashioned.

The beginnings of that transformation, which is to change the believing man's nature from the image of sin to the image of God, are found in conversion when the man is made a partaker of the divine nature. By regeneration and sanctification, by faith and prayer, by suffering and discipline, by the Word and the Spirit, the work goes on till the dream of God has been realized in the Christian heart. Everything that God does in His ransomed children has as its long-range purpose the final restoration of the divine image in human nature. Everything looks forward to the consummation.

In the meantime the Christian himself can work along with God in bringing about the great change. Paul tells us how: "But we all, with open face beholding as in a glass the glory of the Lord, are changed into the same image from glory to glory, even as by the Spirit of the Lord" (2 Corinthians 3:18).

Week 7

PREPARE THE WAY

*. . . prepare the way for the Lord; make
straight in the desert a highway for our God.*

ISAIAH 40:3

These words were spoken by a man of God in a particular time; it has a particular and specific historic setting, and it can be understood that way.

God was preparing a people for the greatest event that ever took place in this world—the manifestation of the Messiah. In order to do that He had to prepare the people morally to understand Him and to receive Him.

That is the historic setting, but remember these words also have application for today because they constitute a spiritual principle which God has laid down and from which He has never varied during the centuries. It is always that way. If God is preparing to bless a man, that man has to get ready.

I know that will shock some people because there is a badly conceived theory abroad that God does it all; all you and I have to do is be born. After that God just picks us up on eagle wings and sweeps us irresistibly through to the crown at last. I cannot imagine how such a notion could ever have lodged itself in heads as small as ours are, but it is there. Consequently, it is necessary to point out that this is an error and that the principle of God's operation is that when He is about to do something unusual for a nation, a church, an individual, He gets that individual or nation or church morally ready. John was sent to do that very thing.

God wills certain things for people—spiritual prosperity, I might call it. Let me say that it consists of about two things: first, clear forgiveness of sin and washing from the same. God's will for everyone who hears the gospel is that we should be forgiven and thoroughly cleansed from sin. Second, we should be filled and walk in the fullness of the Holy Ghost all the days of our life. That will eventuate immediately, of course, fruitfulness, peace of heart, purity of life, and general usefulness to our generation before we go hence to be no more.

WHO PUT JESUS ON THE CROSS?

But he was pierced for our transgressions, he was crushed for our iniquities; the punishment that brought us peace was on him, and by his wounds we are healed.

ISAIAH 53:5

I saiah sums up his message of a substitutionary atonement with the good news that "with his stripes we are healed."

The meaning of these "stripes" in the original language is not a pleasant description. It means to be actually hurt and injured until the entire body is black and blue as one great bruise.

Mankind has always used this kind of bodily laceration as a punitive measure. Society has always insisted upon the right to punish a man for his own wrongdoing. The punishment is generally suited to the nature of the crime. It is a kind of revenge—society taking vengeance against the person who dared flout the rules.

But the suffering of Jesus Christ was not punitive. It was not for Himself and not for punishment of anything that He Himself had done.

The suffering of Jesus was corrective. He was willing to suffer in order that He might correct us and perfect us, so that His suffering might not begin and end in suffering, but that it might begin in suffering and end in healing.

Brethren, that is the glory of the cross! That is the glory of the kind of sacrifice that was for so long in the heart of God! That is the glory of the kind of atonement that allows a repentant sinner to come into peaceful and gracious fellowship with his God and Creator! It began in His suffering and it ended in our healing. It began in His wounds and ended in our purification. It began in His bruises and ended in our cleansing.

What is our repentance? I discover that repentance is mainly remorse for the share we had in the revolt that wounded Jesus Christ, our Lord. Further, I have discovered that truly repentant men never quite get over it, for repentance is not a state of mind and spirit that takes its leave as soon as God has given forgiveness and as soon as cleansing is realized.

That painful and acute conviction that accompanies repentance may well subside and a sense of peace and cleansing come, but even the holiest of justified men will think back over his part in the wounding and the chastisement of the Lamb of God. A sense of shock will still come over him. A sense of wonder will remain—wonder that the Lamb that was wounded should turn His wounds into the cleansing and forgiveness of one who wounded Him.

This brings to mind a gracious moving in many of our evangelical church circles—a willingness to move toward the spiritual purity of heart taught and exemplified so well by John Wesley in a time of spiritual dryness.

In spite of the fact that the word *sanctification* is a good Bible word, we have experienced a period in which evangelical churches hardly dared breathe the word because of the fear of being classified among the "holy rollers."

Not only is the good word *sanctification* coming back, but I am hopeful that what the word stands for in the heart and mind of God is coming back too. The believing Christian, the child of God, should have a holy longing and desire for the pure heart and clean hands that are a delight to his Lord. It was for this that Jesus Christ allowed Himself to be humiliated, maltreated, lacerated. He was bruised, wounded, and chastised so that the people of God could be a cleansed and spiritual people—in order that our minds might be pure and our thoughts pure. This provision all began in His suffering and ends in our cleansing. It began with His open, bleeding wounds and ends in peaceful hearts and calm and joyful demeanor in His people.

IDENTIFIED
WITH CHRIST

*But whoever is united with
the Lord is one with him in spirit.*

1 CORINTHIANS 6:17

Oneness with Christ means to be identified with
Christ, identified with Him in crucifixion. But we
must go on to be identified with Him in resurrection as
well, for beyond the cross is resurrection and the manifestation of His presence.

I would not want to make the mistake of some preach-
ers who have never gotten beyond the message of death,
death, death! They preach it so much that they never get
anyone beyond death into resurrection life and victory.

I recall that when I was a young man and getting along

well spiritually, having been wonderfully filled with the Holy Spirit, I read a book about the cross. In that volume, the author put you on the cross in the first chapter, and you were still hanging on the cross in the last chapter. It was gloomy all the way through—and I had a difficult time shaking that off because it was death, death, death! I was greatly helped at that time by the radiant approach of Dr. A. B. Simpson to the meaning of the cross and death to self. He took one through the meaning of the cross to the understanding that beyond the cross there is resurrection life and power, an identification with a risen Savior and the manifestation of His loving presence.

The old fifteenth-century saint whom we have quoted declared that "God is ingenuous in making us crosses."

Considering that, we have to confess that when some Christians say, "I am crucified with Christ by faith," they are merely using a technical term and are not talking about a cross in reality. But God wants His children to know the cross. He knows that only spiritual good can come to us as a result of our identification with the Lord Jesus. So He is ingenuous in making crosses for us.

The quotation continues:

> He may make them of iron and of lead which are heavy of themselves. He makes some of straw which seem to weigh nothing, but one discovers that they are no less difficult to carry. A cross that appears to be of straw so that

others think it amounts to nothing may be crucifying you through and through. He makes some with gold and precious stones which dazzle the spectators and excite the envy of the public but which crucify no less than the crosses which are more despised.

Christians who are put in high places, Christians who are entrusted with wealth and influence, know something about the kind of cross that may seem dazzling to spectators and excites the envy of the public—but if they know how to take it, it crucifies them no less than the others.

It seems that He makes our crosses of all the things we like the best so that when they turn to bitterness we are able to learn the true measure of eternal values.

It appears, also, that it often pleases God to join physical weakness to this servitude of the Spirit.

"Nothing is more useful than these two crosses together," the quote from the old saint continues. "They crucify a man from head to foot."

I confess that when I read that it came like a shock to my soul, realizing anew that Jesus Christ was crucified from head to foot! When they nailed Him there, He was crucified in every part of His body and there was no part of His holy nature that did not suffer the full intensity of those pains on the cross.

The children of God must be ready for everything the cross brings or we will surely fail the test! It is God's desire to so deal with us about all of the things that the world admires and praises that we will see them in their true light. He will treat us without pity because He desires to raise us without measure—just as He did with His own Son on the cross!

DEAD IN CHRIST

For Christ's love compels us, because we are convinced
that one died for all, and therefore all died. . . . that
those who live should no longer live for themselves.

2 CORINTHIANS 5:14–15

As believers, we are supposed to have died with Jesus Christ our Lord. When we were joined to Him in the new birth, we were joined to His death. When we were joined to His rising again, it should have been plain to us that sin is now a moral incongruity in the life of a Christian.

The sinner sins because he is out there in the world—and he has never died. He is waiting to die and he will die once and later he will die the second death.

But a Christian dies with Christ and dies in Christ and dies along with Christ, so that when he lays his body down at last the Bible says he will not see death.

God will cover the eyes of all Christians when the time comes—they never see death. The Christian stops breathing and there is a burial but he does not see death—for he already died in Christ when Christ died, and he arose with Christ when Christ arose.

That is why sin is a moral incongruity in the life and deportment of the Christian believer. It is a doctrine and theology completely unknown to those whose Christianity is like a button or flower stuck on the lapel—completely external.

I believe the gospel of Jesus Christ saved me completely—therefore He asks me for total commitment. He expects me to be a disciple totally dedicated.

Joined to Jesus Christ, how can we be other than what He is? What He does, we do. Where He leads, we go. This is genuine Christianity!

Sin is now an outrage against holy blood. To sin now is to crucify the Son of God afresh. To sin now is to belittle the blood of atonement. For a Christian to sin now is to insult the holy life laid down. I cannot believe that any Christian wants to sin.

All offenses against God will either be forgiven or avenged—we can take our choice. All offenses against God, against ourselves, against humanity, against human life—all offenses will be either forgiven or avenged. There are two voices—one pleading for vengeance, the other pleading for mercy.

What a terrible thing for men and women to get old and have no prospect, no gracious promise for the long eternity before them.

But how beautiful to come up like a ripe shock of corn and know that the Father's house is open, the doors are wide open and the Father waits to receive His children one after another!

Some years ago one of our national Christian brothers from the land of Thailand gave his testimony in my hearing. He told what it had meant in his life and for his future when the missionaries came with the good news of the gospel of Christ.

He described the godly life of one of the early missionaries and then said, "He is in the Father's house now."

He told of one of the missionary women and the love of Christ she had displayed and then said, "She is in the Father's house now."

What a vision for a humble Christian who only a generation before had been a pagan, worshiping idols and spirits—and now because of grace and mercy he talks about the Father's house as though it were just a step away, across the street.

This is the gospel of Christ—the kind of Christianity I believe in. What joy to discover that God is not mad at us and that we are His children—because Jesus died for us, because the blood of Jesus "speaketh better things than that of Abel" (Hebrews 12:24). What a blessing to find out that the mercy of God speaks louder than the voice of justice. What a hope that makes it possible for the Lord's people to lie down quietly when the time comes and whisper, "Father, I am coming home!"

Oh, we ought to make more of the blood of the Lamb, because it is by the blood that we are saved; by the blood atonement is made.

THE PASSION
OF CHRIST

For the wages of sin is death, but the gift
of God is eternal life in Christ Jesus our Lord.

ROMANS 6:23

The word *passion* now means "sex lust," but back in the early days it meant deep, terrible suffering. That is why they call Good Friday "Passion Tide" and we talk about "the passion of Christ." It is the suffering Jesus did as He made His priestly offering with His own blood for us.

Jesus Christ is God, and all I've said about God describes Christ. He is unitary. He has taken on Himself the nature of man, but God the Eternal Word, who was before man and who created man, is a unitary being and there is no dividing of His substance. And so that Holy

One suffered, and His suffering in His own blood for us was three things. It was infinite, almighty, and perfect.

Infinite means without bound and without limit, shoreless, bottomless, topless forever and ever, without any possible measure or limitation. And so the suffering of Jesus and the atonement He made on that cross under that darkening sky was infinite in its power.

It was not only infinite but *almighty*. It's possible for good men to "almost" do something or to "almost" be something. That is the fix people get in because they are people. But Almighty God is never "almost" anything. God is always exactly what He is. He is the Almighty One. Isaac Watts said about His dying on the cross, "God the mighty Maker died for man the creature's sin." And when God the Almighty Maker died, all the power there is was in that atonement. You never can overstate the efficaciousness of the atonement. You never can exaggerate the power of the cross.

And God is not only infinite and almighty but *perfect*. The atonement in Jesus Christ's blood is perfect; there isn't anything that can be added to it. It is spotless, impeccable, flawless. It is perfect as God is perfect. So Anselm's question, "How dost Thou spare the wicked if Thou art just?" is answered from the effect of Christ's passion. That holy suffering there on the cross and that resurrection from the dead cancels our sins and abrogates our sentence.

Where and how did we get that sentence? We got it by

the application of justice to a moral situation. No matter how nice and refined and lovely you think you are, you are a moral situation—you have been, you still are, you will be. And when God confronted you, God's justice confronted a moral situation and found you unequal, found inequity, found iniquity.

Because He found iniquity there, God sentenced you to die. Everybody has been or is under the sentence of death. I wonder how people can be so jolly under the sentence of death. "The soul that sinneth, it shall die" (Ezekiel 18:20). When justice confronts a moral situation in a man, woman, young person, or anybody morally responsible, then either it justifies or condemns that person. That's how we got that sentence. . . .

But oh, the mystery and wonder of the atonement! The soul that avails itself of that atonement, that throws itself out on that atonement, the moral situation has changed. God has not changed! Jesus Christ did not die to change God; Jesus Christ died to change a moral situation. When God's justice confronts an unprotected sinner that justice sentences him to die. And all of God concurs in the sentence! But when Christ, who is God, went onto the tree and died there in infinite agony, in a plethora of suffering, this great God suffered more than they suffer in hell. He suffered all that they could suffer in hell. He suffered with the agony of God, for everything that God does, He does with all that He is. When God suffered for you, my friend, God suffered to change your moral situation.

WE STAND IN CHRIST'S TRIUMPH

. . . we are more than conquerors through him who loved us.

ROMANS 8:37

The unique thing about the early Christians was their radiant relation to a Person. "The Lord," they called Him tenderly, and when they used the term they gave it its own New Testament meaning. It meant Jesus Christ, who a short while before had been among them but was now gone into the heavens as their High Priest and Advocate.

It was this engrossment with a victorious Person that gave verve and vibrancy to their lives and conviction to their testimony. They bore witness joyously to the One who had lived as a true Man among men. Their testimony was not weakened by the pale cast of metaphysical thought. They knew that Jesus was very Man and very God, and He had died, had been raised from the dead, and had ascended into heaven. They accepted literally His claim to be invested with authority over everything in heaven, earth, and hell. How it could be they never stopped to inquire. They trusted Him absolutely and left the details to their triumphant Lord.

Another marked characteristic of the witness of those first Christians was their insistence that Jesus was Lord and mover in a long-range plan to restore the earth and to bring it again under divine control. He is now sovereign Head of His body, the Church, they declared, and will extend His rule to include the earth and the world in His own good time. Hence they never presented Him as Savior merely. It never occurred to them to invite people to receive "peace of mind" or "peace of soul." Nor did they stop at forgiveness or joy or happiness. They gathered up all these benefits into one Person and preached that Person as the last and highest sum of every good possible to be known and enjoyed in this world or that which is to come. "The same Lord over all," they said, "is rich unto all that call upon him" (Romans 10:12). The seeker must own Him Lord triumphant, not a meek-eyed Lover of their souls only, but Lord above all question or doubt.

Today we hold the same views, but our *emphasis* is not the same. The meek and lowly Jesus has displaced the high and holy Jesus in the minds of millions. The vibrant note of triumph is missing in our witness. A sad weeping Jesus offers us His quiet sympathy in our griefs and temptations, but He appears to be as helpless as we are when the pressure is on. His pale feminine face looks at us from the "holy picture" of the Catholic and the Easter card of the Protestant. We give Him our sympathy, but scarcely our confidence. The helpless Christ of the crucifix and the vacuous-countenanced Christ that looks out in sweet innocence from the walls of our evangelical homes is all one and the same. The Catholics rescue Him by bringing a Queen of Heaven to His aid. But we Protestants have no helper. So we sing pop choruses to cheer our drooping spirits and hold panel discussions in the plaintive hope that someone will come up with the answer to our scarce-spoken complaint.

Well, we already have the answer if we but had the faith and wisdom to turn to it. The answer is Christ Victorious, high over all. He lives forever above the reach of His foes. He has but to speak and it is done; He need but command and heaven and earth obey Him. Within the broad framework of his far-looking plans He tolerates for a time the wild outlawry of a fallen world, but He holds the earth in His hand and can call the nation to judgment whenever He wills.

Yes, Christian pilgrim, we are better off than the sad Church can see. We stand in Christ's triumph. Because He lives we live also. "Thanks be to God, which giveth us the victory through our Lord Jesus Christ" (1 Corinthians 15:57).

REFERENCES

WEEK 1

Day 1—The Hunger of the Wilderness: *The Root of the Righteous* (Camp Hill, PA: Christian Publications, 1955; repr. Chicago: Moody Publishers, 2015), 121–123.

Day 2—Faith Is a Perturbing Thing: *The Root of the Righteous*, 54–56.

Day 3—The Uses of Suffering: *The Root of the Righteous*, 159–162.

Day 4—Taking Time to Know God: *The Root of the Righteous*, 13–15.

WEEK 2

Day 5—No Regeneration without Reformation: *The Root of the Righteous*, 49–52.

Day 6—Be Holy!: *Tozer Speaks*, Volume 2, (Camp Hill, PA: Christian Publications, 1994; repr. Camp Hill, PA: WingSpread Publishers, 2010), 57–59.

Day 7—Bible Taught or Spirit Taught?: *The Root of the Righteous*, 41–44.

Day 8—God Is Easy to Live With: *The Root of the Righteous*, 18–20.

Day 9—True Faith Brings Commitment: *The Root of the Righteous*, 57–59.

Day 10—The Key to Spiritual Power: *I Talk Back to the Devil* (Camp Hill, PA: Christian Publications, 1990; repr. Camp Hill, PA: WingSpread Publishers, 2008), 99–102.

WEEK 3

Day 11—The Terror of the Lord: *The Root of the Righteous*, 46–47.

Day 12—Our Enemy Contentment: *The Root of the Righteous*, 66–68.

Day 13—Stopped Dead in Your Tracks?: *I Talk Back to the Devil*, 55–57.

Day 14—Coddled or Crucified?: *The Early Tozer: A Word in Season* (Camp Hill, PA: Christian Puplications, 1997), 83–84.

Day 15—The Great Disparity: *The Root of the Righteous*, 61–63.

Day 16—The Blessedness of Possessing Nothing: *The Pursuit of God* (Camp Hill, PA: Christian Publications, 1948; repr. Chicago, IL: Moody Publishers, 2015), 28–30.

WEEK 4

Day 17—No One Wants to Die on a Cross: *I Talk Back to the Devil*, 90–93.

Day 18—True Cultivation: *The Pursuit of God*, 75–77.

Day 19—We Must Die If We Would Live: *The Root of the Righteous*, 77–79.

Day 20—The Gaze of the Soul: *The Pursuit of God*, 96–98.

Day 21—Mortify the Flesh: *Success and the Christian: The Cost of Spiritual Maturity* (Camp Hill, PA: Christian Publications, 1994; repr. Chicago, IL: WingSpread Publishers, 2010), 44–46.

Day 22—The Sanctification of Our Desires: *The Root of the Righteous*, 139–141.

WEEK 5

Day 23—No Saviorhood without Lordship: *The Root of the Righteous*, 101-104.

Day 24—Crucified with Christ: *Who Put Jesus on the Cross?* (Camp Hill, PA: Christian Publications, 1976; repr., Camp Hill, PA: WingSpread Publishers, 2009), 137-139.

Day 25—Praise God for the Furnace: *The Root of the Righteous*, 163-165.

Day 26—The Fruits of Obedience: *Paths to Power* (Camp Hill, PA: Christian Publications, 1940; repr. Chicago, IL: Moody Publishers, 2016), 30-32.

Day 27—The Need for Self-Judgment: *Of God and Men* (Camp Hill, PA: Christian Publications, 1948; repr. Chicago, IL: Moody Publishers, 2015), 55-57.

Day 28—The Cross Is a Radical Thing: *The Root of the Righteous*, 73-75.

WEEK 6

Day 29—Following the Lord: *Paths to Power*, 34-37.

Day 30—The Cross Does Interfere: *Of God and Men*, 43-46.

Day 31—God Stands Ready: *I Talk Back to the Devil*, 67-68.

Day 32—"It Will Cost You Nothing": *Christ the Eternal Son* (Camp Hill, PA: Christian Publications, 1982; repr. Chicago, IL: WingSpread Publishers, 2010), 128-130.

Day 33—Raised with Christ: *I Talk Back to the Devil*, 105-107.

Day 34—Christ Is the Pattern: *The Root of the Righteous*, 69-72.

WEEK 7

Day 35—Prepare the Way: *Tozer Speaks to Students:* (Camp Hill, PA: Christian Publications, 1999; repr. Chicago, IL: WingSpread Publishers, 2010), 17-18.

Day 36—The Significance of His Stripes: *Who Put Jesus on the Cross?*, 7-9.

Day 37—Identified with Christ: *I Talk Back to the Devil*, 102-104.

Day 38—Dead in Christ: *Echoes from Eden* (Camp Hill, PA: Christian Publications, 1981; repr. Camp Hill, PA: WingSpread Publishers, 2010), 42-44.

Day 39—The Passion of Christ: *The Attributes of God*, Volume 1 (Camp Hill, PA: Christian Publications, 2003; repr. Chicago, IL: WingSpread Publishers, 2007), 67-70.

Day 40—We Stand in Christ's Triumph: *The Root of the Righteous*, 85-88.

"Like many evangelicals who love the gospel,
I had my doubts about Lent."